UNSOLVED:
The JonBenét Ramsey Murder
25 YEARS LATER

PAULA WOODWARD

City Point Press

City Point Press
P.O. Box 2063
Westport, CT 06880
www.citypointpress.com
(203) 571-0781

Hardcover ISBN 978-1-947951-46-4
eBook ISBN 978-1-947951-47-1

Jacket and book design by Barbara Aronica-Buck

Manufactured in the United States of America

There's no tragedy like the death of a child. Things never get back to the way they were.
> —Dwight D. Eisenhower
> Supreme Commander, Allied Forces, World War II
> US President, January 1953 to January 1961

When your child is murdered, the anger, pain, and grief are compounded by the crushing realization that another person intentionally took the life of someone so precious, so innocent.

To see your child's name on a headstone is impossible.
> —Parents of Murdered Children, Inc.
> Two mothers on their daughters' murders

Reason is not automatic. Those who deny it cannot be conquered by it.
> —Ayn Rand
> Philosopher, Novelist, Playwright, Screenwriter

Logic is the technique by which we add conviction to truth.
> —Jean de la Bruyére
> 17th Century Philosopher and Moralist

It was a time when the air shimmered with the sweet and familiar.
We were laughing.
It's another memory of us I carry.

Steve, thank you.
For your constant belief in me and support
for what you always believed I could do.
Like writing this book.

It's dedicated to you. For your belief in me that still sustains.
Love you. Miss you. Another memory to carry with me.

CONTENTS

Introduction   ix

Chapter 1: John, Jan, and John Andrew Ramsey   1

Chapter 2: Where Are They Now?   9

Chapter 3: Publicity—The First Week   20

Chapter 4: Publicity—Ongoing   37

Chapter 5: Evidence   57

Chapter 6: Evidence—The Ransom Note   79

Chapter 7: Evidence—DNA   86

Chapter 8: Evidence—Family History   96

Chapter 9: Evidence—Burke, Fruit Cocktail, Interview Hysteria,
    Federal Judge Ruling   109

Chapter 10: Evidence—Ramsey Grand Jury   120

Chapter 11: Evidence—District Attorney Exoneration   126

Chapter 12: Insider Insights   133

Chapter 13: Continuing Interest   139

Chapter 14: JonBenét: Who She Was   143

Endnotes   165

Acknowledgments   167

Website   171

Documents   173

Index   205

INTRODUCTION

In 1996, the news of the murder of a six-year-old girl ricocheted through the world, splintering truth and cementing conviction that the parents of JonBenét Ramsey of Boulder, Colorado, killed their daughter. There was little doubt, based on the initial news reporting, that it could have been anyone other than her parents.

Here's why.

The initial information in that first week, released by law enforcement authorities, was part of a strategy by certain Boulder police officers to convict the parents through public opinion. The information was deliberately incorrect, distorted, and was devised to take the focus off an initially botched police investigation. It also advanced the police theory about the murder—that the parents killed their daughter—and justified to them any and all sharing of inaccurate information to the media and the public in those first days. It has continued for twenty-five years.

None of the initial investigators on the Ramsey case had homicide experience. There was no homicide department in the Boulder Police Department because there weren't enough homicides to justify one. JonBenét Ramsey's murder was the first murder that year in the town. The Boulder Police Department still doesn't have a homicide department.

Here are the facts:

Twenty-five years ago, JonBenét Ramsey was tortured, murdered, and found in a basement storage room in her home on the day after Christmas, December 26, 1996. It happened in Boulder, Colorado.

The circumstances surrounding her murder were devastating and bizarre. She was reported kidnapped by her parents early that morning. A two-and-a-half-page ransom note was left inside the home. The note, addressed to her father, said she'd been taken.

Her body was discovered seven hours later, not by the police, but by her father. Why didn't the police find her body in their search of the home? A first-responding officer explained in his police report why he didn't open the door to the room where her body had been left.

Law enforcement settled immediately on John and Patsy as the killers and set out to prove it. The fact that JonBenét was involved in child beauty pageants and there was video of her performing in them was widely publicized. Talk show entertainment focused on the pageants, the publicized video of JonBenét, and whether her parents were acting responsibly in this choice for their child. Critics questioned the focus on beauty and sexuality for young children. JonBenét was a naturally beautiful child with blond hair and blue eyes. Opinions were strong enough about child pageants that on January 19, 1997, *The Kansas City Star* headlined an editorial: "Pillars of the Community? These Parents are Creeps."

The first book I wrote, *We Have Your Daughter: The Unsolved Murder of JonBenét Ramsey Twenty Years Later,* was published in 2016. That book examines the Ramsey case investigation, the hysteria of the media coverage, public reaction, and the decisions of those in power who were affected by the focused and erratic publicity storm. It also reports, for the first time, the intention by police to leak incorrect data to the media and public about the Ramsey family.

My new book is *Unsolved: The JonBenét Ramsey Murder 25 Years Later.* This book refocuses and expands on the many aspects of the intentional agenda by police who manipulated evidence, ignored inconvenient evidence, and spread untruths in their campaign to convict Patsy and John Ramsey as their daughter's killers. These actions had a profound impact on the direction, fairness, and honesty of the case. The added scrutiny provides new insight.

I talk with editors from Denver newspapers who worked at the time JonBenét's body was discovered and after and find out their reactions to the intentional misinformation campaign. I trace the huge number of newspapers and television networks throughout the country that published this false material and examine how it affected our perceptions of whether the Ramseys killed their daughter. The Ramseys believe Boulder police investigators tried to "frame" them. You can decide.

With hindsight, there are new truths and more input available about the evidence in the case. I investigate and expand on the conspiracy by law enforcement in the last twenty-five years to implicate Patsy and John Ramsey in their daughter's sadistic death.

For this book, I interviewed a homicide detective about the planned leaks and the evidence. The detective has thirty years of homicide experience in a major metropolitan city. He has worked on hundreds of homicides and is familiar with the Ramsey case. He has never worked in Boulder and has the credibility of an outsider for this particular case. He won't allow his name to be used because of the negative impacts of this case. He comments about what is valuable and what isn't with the evidence available, and he has observations about the media disinformation plan as it unfolds.

The police on the Ramsey case spent untold dollars and acted without supervision in their zeal to convict the Ramseys. I believe it's imperative to expose public servants whose job is to help, but who instead harm. Those are the types of stories I have reported as an investigative reporter for more than thirty years.

Unsolved includes documents and research from the twenty-five years I've spent on the case. I began reporting on it the day after JonBenét's body was found. I was an investigative reporter for television station KUSA TV in Denver. I also wrote and reported during that time for *The Denver Post* and the *Rocky Mountain News* as part of a business partnership.

Documents utilized for evaluating the evidence in the case and the strategic and deliberate mistruths and leaks by the Boulder Police Department and Boulder District Attorney's Office include a re-examination of newspaper archives from *Newspapers.com, The Denver Post,* the *Rocky Mountain News,* and the *Boulder Daily Camera.* National television evening news broadcasts for ABC, NBC, CBS, and CNN were examined using the Vanderbilt University Television News Archives in Nashville, Tennessee.

Other sources of information used to develop new facts on the evidence and misinformation include details from a 3,000-page JonBenét Ramsey Murder Book Summary Index. The index is not publicly available. It was something I was able to obtain. It is a summary of thousands of Boulder police reports. The FBI, Colorado Bureau of Investigation, and the Boulder Sheriff's Department contributed to these reports which are listed in the book with the following identifiers: BPD Report #, and a listed number. The JonBenét Ramsey Murder Book Summary Index was organized and prepared by the Boulder District Attorney's Office. The report numbers may have changed.

Information from the JonBenét Ramsey Murder Book Summary Index has been published only once before, in my first book.

John, his wife, Jan, and his son John Andrew update us twenty-five years later, both about themselves and about JonBenét with stunning candor.

I have re-interviewed numerous people who had various jobs and points of view in this case about what has changed and what hasn't in the last twenty-five years. Included are people from the District Attorney's Office in Boulder and the Boulder Police Department.

A source provided me with a 1,000-page file of all Boulder Police Department officers involved in the Ramsey case and a 182-page confidential Boulder Police Department Master Witness List. I have used information from both.

All documents reviewed for this book have been verified.

Some of the law enforcement interviewed for this book have asked that their names not be used. These people are well known to me and have met my editor's tough requirements for allowing anonymity.

The case continues to defy neutrality. Those who criticize or question the "Ramseys Did It" theory become targets on entertainment talk shows.

Twenty-five years later, the case still has tremendous power to affect adversely.

During this long and chaotic time, I have been criticized by a few shrill accusers for allegedly "becoming too close to the Ramseys." That's wrong. What is accurate is I was one of the few reporters who were able to get interviews with Patsy and John Ramsey. What is compelling and became routine is that reporters who interviewed the Ramseys were accused of siding with the family. I haven't. I interviewed the Ramseys because it was critically important to get their side of the story. That is one of the basic tenets of journalism. At the very least, get two sides of the story and more if you can. The more views and perspectives obtained on this troublesome case and the more that can be learned, then the less likely corruption can continue to hide. The story isn't over, and I will continue to report on the Ramsey family. As of now, it's still an unsolved case. It is possible, after twenty-five years, that a suspect could be arrested at any time.

Personal items of JonBenét's and new photographs of her are shown to better understand her loss to her family and perhaps to the rest of us.

CHAPTER 1:
JOHN, JAN, AND JOHN ANDREW RAMSEY

John and Jan Ramsey were married in 2014, eight years after Patsy Ramsey died from ovarian cancer.

John Ramsey went from a mansion to a mobile home. From a self-made millionaire to living a good portion of his life paycheck-to-paycheck, he still works at seventy-seven years old. He lives in southern Utah. He is involved with an air tour company that does scenic tours and his wife, Jan, works with hospitality apparel and uniforms. He says he does not have the money to retire.

He spent his savings twenty-five years ago on his own investigation into who killed his daughter. He and his attorneys believed "that the police and the district attorney were incapable."

He ran out of money because he was unable to get a job. The Ramsey case investigators' deliberate plan to leak untrue information to an eager media succeeded in destroying his reputation. He speaks about interviewing with one company who told him he was "very well-qualified, but we can't hire you. The backlash to our company, which is publicly held, would be too detrimental." His words.

He remarried eight years after Patsy died after a long battle with ovarian cancer. His new wife, Jan, is a missionary's daughter. They met through mutual friends.

Jan thought she knew about the Ramsey case and realizes now she didn't truly understand the dynamic of JonBenét Ramsey: the murder, the devastation, the frenzy, the mystery, and how it affected who she was marrying: "A couple of days before we got married in 2014, he was pacing back and forth, and peeking out the window and concerned about people that might be trying to take pictures. He asked me not to take a walk down to the beach. He didn't want people photographing me, and I thought 'Oh this poor man. He's so great in every way, but he's been traumatized and I'm going to just have to overlook this,' because I thought he was a little neurotic or something. But lo and behold, we ended up in the newspaper. Front page in the *Globe* and the *National Enquirer* directly after our wedding. And sure enough, he was right. People were still very interested in his life, and I was dumbfounded that our wedding was of any interest to anybody outside our family and friends. I have learned so much since then about the interest. It doesn't end. First there was the twenty-year anniversary and now there's the twenty-fifth-year anniversary of his daughter's murder."

For John and his son John Andrew, being diplomatic, their guidepost for these last twenty-five years, no longer matters. Being carefully polite is no longer an answer: "The real story here is not that a child, my daughter, was murdered. Sadly, that happens way too often in our country. The real story is what was done to our family by a careless and incompetent police department. They have the capacity to do great harm. They can destroy lives, they can destroy futures, and with absolutely no accountability. And to me, that is the real story."

John continues in his relentless quest to find a killer in part because he wants to make sure Boulder police investigators continue to work the case. "I don't want those in charge of the case to park it in a death file and let dust collect on it. Somebody's got to do it. The continuing publicity helps to keep the pressure on them."

With the renewed quest for equal justice and standards for use of force with police departments, John believes there are differing levels of misconduct across police forces. "Police hurt people in ways including devastating loss with a wrongful death. The misbehavior and illegal misconduct is there constantly. It has certainly happened to us and it's happened to other people, too. Serious policing is a problem in this country. And I don't necessarily have a solution. Pay them better, train them better, and be more selective in choosing them. Get rid of the gun-carrying bullies." That has become his most consistent message twenty-five years later. He is very aware of those police officers who helped his family and how they are the examples of honor in being a police officer. "The ones who helped us are not exceptions with police officers. There are many good officers, but not the ones who were part of our case."

John Andrew has had a lot of time to absorb and watch what is happening with his father's continuing defense of the family and search for a killer: "We were a private family whose child and sister was just murdered. It's incredibly frustrating and maddening that we've been put in this position of not only fighting for our reputation and our character, but also trying to get justice for JonBenét. Yet we've been put in this unbelievable situation of trying to go out and find her killer. It's ludicrous that the family has to go out there and do it themselves. It just doesn't make any sense. It's incredibly wrong. We continue to be victimized. I think of my dad. He's been doing this for twenty-five years."

John freely and willingly admits his faith is how he has lived and survived in life since his daughter Beth was killed in a car accident, JonBenét was murdered, and Patsy ultimately lost her battle with cancer. Does he believe he'll see them again? "Yes. Oh yes. Absolutely, I believe this will happen." That's one of his certainties. "There's got to be more to life than what we experience here. If not, then life's a pretty cruel joke."

He doesn't believe in peace on earth: "I don't know if you ever have peace in this world. Really have peace. There are times when I'm sad and remember and regret my losses, but you've got to work at it and move ahead. Nobody said life was easy."

He, Patsy, and JonBenét's nine-year old brother Burke, who was in the home when his sister was killed and was considered a suspect at various times during that twenty-five years, lived with different friends in Boulder after they buried JonBenét. "We came back to help Boulder police find the monster who killed JonBenét. We quickly found out that we were the monster according to them."

They moved back to Atlanta for Burke to continue with school. Atlanta was home. They had moved to Boulder for John's business, but had planned for it to be a temporary move and always intended to return to Atlanta. Once they had moved back, they looked for a home to buy and found they were continuing to deal with grief, which they expected, but they were unaware of some unexpected realities that surfaced even with a simple search for a home: "The homes we looked at couldn't have a basement because of the horror we had in Boulder. We were also very aware when we were looking for a home to buy, where the media could hide out to keep track of us. That was a factor in what house we bought—whether the media could find a place to hide and watch us." They moved again to Charlevoix, Michigan, where they had spent summers for years, in time for Burke's junior year. "He had so many friends from being there every summer. It was a good decision."

John ran for state representative in Northern Michigan and met some "wonderful people who really wanted what's best for state government." And he learned that politics wasn't for him. "I learned that the politics side was dark, dirty, just nasty. I needed to get back to what I thought was the nice clean world of business."

He misses Patsy and reflects on what the twenty-five years since their daughter was so horribly murdered would mean to Patsy. "I think she would continue to be pretty resilient. She was a strong woman so she would have been focused on her family, Burke, and me. I'm sure she would continuously make sure that we were all trying to get our lives back on track."

Even in the seven short years she's been with him, Jan Ramsey lives the continuing turmoil: "I feel like I'm his firewall. People who can't reach him go through me. And I will have the press calling me, investigators calling me, people with tips calling me. Creepy people are emailing me. I even have a file labeled 'mean or crazy people' because who knows what leads might be in that file.

"I think John is very worn out with it. I think sometimes it beats the stuffing out of him. And while there is still fight in him, he finds it more difficult to hope. Every time we think something really good might be happening, he is just a lot less excited, because he's seen so much disappointment in the solving of this crime over the years. He has a lessening of hope which is difficult when we always want to be more optimistic."

John Andrew works in healthcare technology sales. He points to how normal his family is. How they are all living their lives, contributing to society, and being responsible citizens. And how they are continuing to stir up the case, which is "not really a smart thing for guilty people to do. We do it because we're not guilty of killing JonBenét. We're genuinely trying to find her killer."

John says JonBenét's brother Burke is part of the normalcy in the family. "He finished up high school in northern Michigan, so he likes it there and has a lot of friends there. He loves the summers, which are great. We all like spending time there in the summer. It's a very Norman Rockwell scene living there. Burke even likes those really cold winters because he snowboards and skis."

He worries most about what effect JonBenét's death has on Burke:

"He lost his sister through horrible events. He lost his mother when he was eighteen. He lost his half-sister, Beth, when he was just five years old. Yet he's doing well, very well. He's a software developer and has been working for the same company for six to eight years. He's highly valued by them and doing well. Patsy and I were told by a child psychologist after this happened that children have an ability to compartmentalize things, put them into a different compartment, and get on with life. He said the accumulated grief may resurface for Burke when he's older. So that's always a worry. He's doing great. I'm proud of him as I am of all of my children. They really struggled under some tough circumstances and they are really good people."

Who does John think killed his daughter? "I don't know. I don't know. I subscribe to [former FBI profiler] John Douglas's assessment that this was someone who was either angry at me or jealous of me. This was not about JonBenét. This was about trying to hurt me, which was a heavy burden. I told Douglas, 'I can't imagine ever meeting anybody that mad at me.' He said, 'You may not even know him. He may have obsessed to this point of madness from a distance.'"

Jan thinks the answer to find a killer is in DNA. "I kinda think we're close to it. I do. Because of the DNA. Because John Andrew has gotten involved in driving this more, keeping track of it."

They all know what toll the case has on them: "Losing your daughter and having to go out and talk about this endlessly, digging through all the nuances of what has occurred. I don't know how my dad is able to continue," says John Andrew.

Jan sees first-hand the effects of continuing to work the case and defend the family. "There are times when it visits us in a more intense way for a prolonged time. And that's when this wound, this scabbing in his heart, gets much worse and sometimes it's this drippy, miserable cloud we live under."

The reality for John and Jan is this, according to Jan. "For the most part, we have a wonderful life. We have great things going on. It is a very happy, sweet marriage that we have."

John continues to cooperate in searches for killers and to keep pressure on Boulder police because of the deep feeling that he failed as a father to his daughter, JonBenét. "I'm her father. I always swore to protect her. And the time she needed me most, I wasn't there. I can't ever forget that."

CHAPTER 2:

WHERE ARE THEY NOW?

Patsy Ramsey (PR): (inaudible) police.
911: (inaudible)
PR: 755 Fifteenth Street
911: What is going on there ma'am?
PR: We have a kidnapping...Hurry, please
911: Explain to me what is going on, ok?
PR: We have a...There's a note left and our daughter is gone
911: A note was left and your daughter is gone?
PR: Yes.
911: How old is you daughter?
PR: She is six years old she is blond...six years old
911: How long ago was this?
PR: I don't know. Just found a note a note and my daughter is missing
911: Does it say who took her?
PR: What?
911: Does it say who took her?
PR: No I don't know it's there...there is a ransom note here.
911: It's a ransom note.
PR: It says S.B.T.C. Victory...please
911: Ok, what's your name? Are you...
PR: Patsy Ramsey...I am the mother. Oh my God. Please.
911: I'm...Ok, I'm sending an officer over, ok?
PR: Please.
911: Do you know how long she's been gone?
PR: No, I don't, please, we just got up and she's not here.
    Oh my God Please.
911: Ok.
PR: Please send somebody.
911: I am, honey.
PR: Please send somebody.
911: I am, honey.
PR: Please.
911: Take a deep breath (inaudible).
PR: Hurry, hurry, hurry (inaudible).
911: Patsy? Patsy? Patsy? Patsy? Patsy?

This is the transcript of Patsy Ramsey's call to 911 on December 26, 1996, at approximately 5:52 a.m.

To understand how seriously botched the initial investigation was, it is necessary to focus on what the responding officers failed to do. At the same time, I'll update the officers who were of most interest twenty-five years ago.

OFFICER RICK FRENCH ARRIVES 6:00 A.M.

It was freezing cold and dark outside the Ramsey home when the first responder, Officer Rick French, arrived in answer to Patsy's frantic 911 call that her daughter had been kidnapped. French spent his time in the home, interviewing both parents and searching the home for anything unusual. The search took time.

The Ramsey home included four stories and encompassed 7,000 square feet. It had been remodeled while the family lived there and had what some felt was a confusing layout.

As the first responder, Officer French was responsible for ensuring that the home was searched. During his search, he didn't open the door to the basement storage room where JonBenét's body was, so he didn't find her body. He left at 10:00 a.m. with the other officers except for one detective, and went to write his police report. He returned to the home with a large number of officers when the body was discovered at approximately 1:06 p.m. He then resumed writing his police report, turning in a three-and-a-half-page report at 11:44 p.m. This is his written explanation for not finding JonBenét's body during his search of the home. It's in his police report: "In the basement I attempted to open the door leading to the area where Jonbenet [*sic*] was ultimately found but it was secured by a wooden latch above the door. The door opened inward and I was looking for access out of the house. Since the door could not have been used for that purpose, and it was latched closed, I did not open it."

He didn't open the door. He didn't find her body.

One of his responsibilities as first arriving officer was to start and keep a crime scene entry log, which tracks the arrival and departure of all law enforcement. The crime scene entry log must be signed upon entry and exit by each law officer. It is a precise instrument and investigative tool. Yet the crime scene entry log for the Ramsey home has several arrival and departure times for law enforcement.

Officer French had no homicide experience.

Update: Officer Rick French retired and left the Boulder Police Department within the last three years. He moved out of state.

OFFICER PAUL REICHENBACH ARRIVES 6:02 A.M.

Officer Reichenbach's responsibility was to search the outside of the home. He submitted a one-paragraph police report that did not mention whether he found any footprints. Officer Reichenbach did a brief search inside the home and did not find the child's body.

He was later debriefed on his police report to obtain additional information and during that debriefing and a later search warrant, he stated he "did not believe there was snow on the sidewalks." The relevance of this is that it contradicts a deliberate and incorrect report leaked by two other police officers.

Officer Reichenbach was questioned by supervisors in that unusual debriefing for writing an incomplete police report (one paragraph) and for not conducting a thorough search outside the home.

Officer Reichenbach had no homicide experience.

Update: Officer Reichenbach recently resigned from the Boulder Police Department and currently works as a civilian with Boulder Photo Radar.

COMMANDER-SERGEANT BOB WHITSON
ON-CALL SUPERVISOR ARRIVES: 9:15 A.M.

Whitson arrives at the home, conducts a brief investigation, and leaves at 9:45 a.m., releasing other officers from the scene, and leaving Detective Linda Arndt in charge.

He admits fault for releasing the officers when they should have stayed to support Detective Arndt.

He says he should have cleared the home and instructed that it remain clear of all non-law-enforcement personnel. (Friends of the Ramseys were arriving at the home to provide support. In total, eighteen non-law-enforcement people were in the home that morning, including John and Patsy).

He says he should have "ensured for himself the home had been searched and photographed, even though he was told it had been" before he left to go to the police station.

Commander-Sergeant Whitson had no homicide experience.

Update: Commander-Sergeant Whitson retired from the Boulder Police Department in 2005. He got his PhD in Criminal Justice in 2011. He has moved out of state and is teaching. He wrote a book about the case that was published in 2016 and said the killer was an intruder and a psychopath.

DETECTIVE LINDA ARNDT: ARRIVAL TIMES VARY ACCORDING TO THE CRIME SCENE LOG: 8:10 A.M., 8:11 A.M., 8:30 A.M.

DETECTIVE FRED PATTERSON: ARRIVAL TIMES VARY ACCORDING TO THE CRIME SCENE LOG: 8:10 A.M., 8:11 A.M., 8:30 A.M.

Both detectives were to report immediately to the scene when they were notified within minutes of Patsy Ramsey's 911 call. They both chose not to report to the scene, but to instead go to the police station for documents. More than an hour and a half after they were notified, they arrived at the scene. As the detectives at the crime scene, they were supposed to be in charge.

They both interviewed Patsy and John Ramsey when they arrived at the home. Despite stopping at the police department, they had only one tape recorder between them. None of the interviews with the Ramseys were recorded.

Detective Patterson left at 9:45 a.m. with Commander Whitson. He was in charge of the scene with Detective Arndt and should have stayed, according to homicide protocol.

Detective Arndt was left on her own with approximately eighteen people in the home, including Patsy and John. None of the eighteen was law enforcement, but instead were friends of the Ramsey family. The fact that the detective was left alone defies all established police protocol. Lab personnel, detectives, and whoever else would be helpful to the case should have been in the home and the only people in the home.

Detective Arndt directed John Ramsey and a friend to search the home and he was the person who found his daughter's body and moved it upstairs. That was again a gross violation of protocol and destroyed evidence that was with the child's body. Detective Arndt then moved the child's body again which she shouldn't have done.

Detective Arndt's police report was turned in thirteen days after JonBenét's murder. Police reports on homicides are specifically required to be turned in within twenty-four hours, and at the maximum forty-eight hours. No one enforced the time restraints with Detective Arndt to turn in her report on time.

Neither of the detectives had homicide experience.

Update: Detective Arndt resigned from the Boulder Police Department in 1999. She sued the department and the police chief for violation of her free speech rights, but lost.

Update: Detective Patterson retired several years ago and lives out of state.

HOMICIDE DETECTIVE LOU SMIT

In March of 1997, Detective Smit was hired by the Boulder District Attorney's Office with approval of the Boulder Police Department to bring in outside expertise to the Ramsey case. Smit had worked on more than 200 homicide cases in the Colorado Springs area. The suggestion for his hiring came from Boulder police.

He initially believed the Ramseys were guilty of killing JonBenét, but changed his mind after studying the evidence. The police department had welcomed him when he first started to work with them, but vilified him with derogatory public leaks after he believed an intruder killed JonBenét. He resigned from the job in 1998 saying the case was going in the wrong direction.

Update: Smit died of colon cancer in 2010.

COMMANDER JOHN ELLER: IN CHARGE OF THE RAMSEY INVESTIGATION

Commander Eller was ultimately removed from the case. Questions were asked in the media on why he had not requested interviews with the Ramseys when their daughter's body was found, why he threatened to withhold the body the next day if the parents didn't come to the police station to be interviewed, why he did not control the deliberately erroneous information that was released to the public, and why he did not follow basic homicide protocol. He did not report immediately to the crime scene or the police department when notified at 8:10 a.m. the day the body was found, because he said he had a sick relative.

Commander Eller was removed as commander of the Ramsey case in October 1997. He resigned and moved to Southern Florida in a suburb of Miami. He had moved from Southern Florida when he joined Boulder Police Department years before.

Commander Eller had no homicide experience.

Update: Eller is currently living in southern Florida. He applied for a police chief job in Cocoa Beach, Florida, after leaving Boulder police, but said he did not get the job.

DETECTIVE STEVE THOMAS: ONE OF THE INITIAL DETECTIVES ON THE CASE

Detective Thomas was a narcotics detective in Boulder. He was one of the initial detectives on the case. He left the department in 1998 and co-wrote a book with a published author about the murder. He was sued by the Ramseys for content in that book and his publisher paid the Ramseys as part of the legal settlement. He was criticized by Boulder District Attorney Alex Hunter for using confidential case information in that book while the case was still active. Thomas believed Patsy Ramsey killed her daughter because of bedwetting. Evidence proved JonBenét didn't wet her bed even though her underwear was urine-stained. In spite of the evidence that JonBenét didn't wet her bed, Thomas testified for a 2003 civil pre-trial hearing that Patsy killed Jon-Benét because of bedwetting. A federal judge hearing that civil case, singled him out for criticism about his testimony. In a civil deposition, he admitted knowing about the agenda to leak false information against the Ramseys. He admitted to being a source, while still working on the active homicide case, for an error-ridden *Vanity Fair* article published in September of 1997.

Detective Thomas had no homicide experience.

Update: Thomas worked as a carpenter after leaving the department and advertised as a paid speaker on the Ramsey case. He sold residential real estate in Florida and currently works for a mortgage company there.

BOULDER POLICE CHIEF TOM KOBY

Chief Koby was in charge of the department when JonBenét Ramsey was killed.

He was criticized in the media for lacking leadership, failing to control the Ramsey case, not bringing in offered outside homicide expertise from Denver and Aurora police departments, and not offering adequate training for his officers. A few weeks after the investigation he held an invited-media-only news briefing. His lack of expertise was underscored when he said, after consulting other police departments, they told him the investigation was handled "just right."

Boulder Police Chief Koby had no homicide experience.

Update: Chief Koby announced his retirement from Boulder police in November of 1997. He worked in the Boulder City Manager's Office from May 1998 until he retired at the end of 1998. He originally moved his family to a location north of Boulder, Colorado.

COMMANDER MARK BECKNER

Commander Beckner was the longest-serving commander in the Ramsey investigation. He became involved in the case three weeks after JonBenét was murdered while interviewing the first responders about problems with their reports and initial investigations. In June of 1997, he was appointed lead investigator on the Ramsey case. He succeeded Chief Koby as Boulder police chief in 1998 and retired in March of 2014. He was criticized in the media for lacking knowledge on the Ramsey case after a Reddit.com question and answer interview in 2015 where several of the questions he answered did not reflect accurate case information. The interview was withdrawn from the site after a few days.[1]

Commander Beckner had no homicide experience.

Update: He lives north of Boulder and spends some of his retirement refereeing basketball.

DISTRICT ATTORNEY ALEX HUNTER

Alex Hunter served for twenty-eight years as district attorney in Boulder. Even before the Ramsey murder, Hunter was criticized by other district attorneys in the metro Denver area for lacking leadership, failing to take cases to trial, and for not being involved in the day-to-day running of his office. He spoke often of the terrible relations between the police case investigators and his own office, but did little to correct the situation. He complained of misconduct, out-of-control egos, and violation of active investigation protocols with leaking while he was actively leaking too. Hunter was removed from an active advisory role in the Ramsey grand jury by then Colorado Governor Roy Romer in 1998. When the JonBenét murder happened, Hunter continued his vacation in Hawaii for nine days before returning to Boulder. He was accused of leaking to the tabloids.

Update: Hunter retired in 2000. Boulder did not have term limits while he was in office. Currently, Hunter spends time in both Hawaii and Boulder.

DISTRICT ATTORNEY MARY LACY

Mary Lacy succeeded DA Alex Hunter. She was elected in 2000. She was a long-time attorney at the Boulder District Attorney's Office, highly regarded, and specialized in sexual assault. In 2008, Lacy exonerated John and Patsy Ramsey as suspects in their daughter's death based on new touch DNA found inside the waist band of the child's previously untested long johns. That DNA *matched* DNA taken from the child's panties in 1996 and was not a match to either John or Patsy Ramsey or any other Ramsey family members. Lacy asked for the new testing after analyzing where new DNA could be found. She was criticized for her actions by those who believed the Ramseys killed their daughter. She became the subject of numerous entertainment talk shows. She did not run for re-election in 2009.

Update: Lacy joined a Boulder law firm and has led a low-key life, living in both Boulder and Arizona.

Some of the initial key people in the investigation left at various times during their careers. Others stayed until retirement. The remaining two original case officers still with Boulder police are in charge of what remains of the Ramsey investigation.

CHAPTER 3:

PUBLICITY—THE FIRST WEEK

Patsy and John Ramsey married in 1980. Patsy died of ovarian cancer in 2006.

Why, after twenty-five years, are people still so certain that either:

Patsy Ramsey tortured and killed her daughter, very possibly stun-gunning her twice, then sexually assaulting her, finally using a garrote to choke her to unconsciousness twice, and hitting her so hard that the blow caved in her skull; then, writing a ransom note to cover up what she'd done; or *an outsider tortured and killed the little girl*, very possibly stun-gunning her twice, then sexually assaulting her, finally using a garrote to choke her to unconsciousness twice, and hitting her so hard that the blow caved in her skull; then, writing a ransom note or leaving behind a pre-written note?

Publicity from the first week after the murder formed a solid base for these beliefs. The continuing and, yes, entertaining speculation of who killed the girl and the emerging photos and video of JonBenét performing at child beauty pageants cemented public opinion against the family.

JonBenét was in a stratosphere of her own. The gory details and the reality of how she died and fought to live, the pain and horror she endured in her last minutes of living, hadn't been made public. The sexual assault, the strangulation to unconsciousness then revived, the blow that caved in her skull, even the likelihood of being stun gunned seemed unreal and could be relegated there.

Deflecting the child's death became part of the fascination. It was far less painful and infinitely more captivating to watch her pageant videos on television than to think about her death. "How do you think she looks?" "What about her makeup?" "I had no idea children were dressed like this." "What's with these beauty pageants for children?"

But nowhere was there more damage done than from the continuing coverage of that first week of news coverage after her death. With the deliberate misinformation campaign, here's what you would find out about the case by reading your newspaper or watching television news that week.[2] The headlines written here are flat-out wrong:

Monday, December 30, 1996 Boulder Police News Conference

    No Danger from a Killer on the Loose.

    Patsy Ramsey did not give DNA.

Boulder police had a news conference to update media and the public on the case. The Boulder public information officer said, "DNA was taken from the Ramseys, but not from Patsy Ramsey." "I assume it's because she is still extremely grief-stricken . . ."

That's wrong.

Look at the police report from two days earlier on Saturday, December 28, 1996:

    3:50 p.m. Melinda Bennett Ramsey gives her DNA.
and gives her blood, hair samples and fingerprints.

    4:09 p.m. John Bennett Ramsey gives his DNA.
He gives blood, hair sample and fingerprints.

    4:37 p.m. Patricia "Patsy" Ramsey gives her DNA.

    4:37 p.m. blood draw.

    4:42 p.m. hair samples.

    4:50 p.m. fingerprints.

PCR P96-21871
page 2

At approximately 3:50 pm, Detective Gosage and I met with **Melinda Bennett Ramsey**, dob/11-14-71 (the half-sister of JonBonet) in the BCSO Records Section fingerprint/photo room. Melinda Bennett Ramsey was friendly/cooperative/talkative, and samples were obtained. A photo was taken, and some basic personal information was obtained.

> 3:50 pm blood draw
> 3:55 pm hair samples
> 4:00 pm fingerprints

At approximately 4:09 pm, Detective Gosage and I met with **John Bennett Ramsey**, dob/11-14-71 (the father of JonBonet) in the BCSO Records Section fingerprint/photo room. John Bennett Ramsey was cooperative and reserved, and samples were obtained. A photo was taken, and some basic personal information was obtained. John Bennett Ramsey had present **David L. Williams** of David L. Williams, Inc., **Private Investigations**, 150 E. 10th Ave., Denver, Co 80203, 832-5113, who observed the proceedings.

> 4:09 pm blood draw
> 4:16 pm hair samples
> 4:24 pm fingerprints

At approximately 4:37 pm, Detective Gosage and I met with **Patricia "Patsy" Ramsey**, dob/12-29-56 (the mother of JonBonet) in the BCSO Records Section fingerprint/photo room. Patricia Ramsey was cooperative in our requests, but was crying/sobbing, withdrawn, and non-speaking, and unsteady on her feet. Samples were obtained without incident. A photo was taken, and some basic personal information was obtained. Patricia Ramsey had present **John F. Stavely, attorney**, 1900 15th Street, Boulder, Co 80302, 546-1363, who observed the proceedings.

> 4:37 pm blood draw
> 4:42 pm hair samples
> 4:50 pm fingerprints

During this processing, Patricia Ramsey sobbed/cried, and during fingerprinting asked Detective Gosage "Will this help find who killed my baby?", and made the statement "I did not murder my baby."

1 143

Boulder police report on Ramsey DNA testing: Saturday, December 28, 1996. This page of the report lists the DNA testing of Melinda Ramsey, John Ramsey, and Patsy Ramsey. Written by: Detective Steve Thomas. Detective Ron Gosage assisted.

Included in the police report are Patsy's comments: "During this processing, Patsy Ramsey sobbed/cried and asks, 'Will this help me find who killed my baby?'" And "I did not murder my baby." Both quotes were later leaked to the media in a context that was critical of the grieving mother.

"Patsy Ramsey did not give DNA" was reported in newspapers throughout the country, including Florida and Colorado.

But what was especially telling was that "Patsy Ramsey" was singled out as the person in the family who had not given DNA when she actually did two days before.

For twenty-five years, the investigation has centered on Patsy Ramsey. Was this the first shot investigators took in the campaign to smear her for her short remaining life? Patsy died of ovarian cancer in 2006, ten years after her daughter was murdered. She was diagnosed in July of 1993.

The Monday, December 30, news conference by Boulder police didn't end with phony DNA information. More false information was forthcoming. This information was repeated throughout the first week of media coverage.

The police spokeswoman stated, "Authorities investigating the death in Boulder say the public is in no danger from a killer on the loose." "There is no need for concern." "I'm not going to confirm or deny whether anyone is still out there."

Says the homicide detective I interviewed for his insights on this case: "Basically it turns the light back on the family. This early in the investigation, Boulder isn't in a position to prove or support that statement. It's wrong. It's not true at this time. It hurts the investigation. It can be brought up at trial to show hasty and unfounded bias."

This detective worked in homicides for thirty years for a major metropolitan police department. He agreed to provide perspective on homicide investigations and media effects on those investigations. He provides an objective look at the case and has no ties to Boulder. As noted before, he wouldn't allow his name to be used.

What's the information the public, especially parents in Boulder, wanted to know right then that Monday? "How safe are my children?"

And that's what the Boulder police news conference was trying to accomplish whether they could prove it or not and whether it was accurate or not.

The news conference statements left little doubt as to where the investigation was going and who police believe killed JonBenét.

On Monday, *The Daily News* in New York carried the Boulder police spokeswoman "No Cause for Concern" statement to its logical conclusion. **"Police would not call the 53-year-old father a suspect. But tellingly, they said the public is in no danger from a killer on the loose."** *The Daily News* December 26, 1996

Tuesday, December 31, 1996
No DNA from Patsy.
No Danger from a Killer on the Loose.

On Tuesday, at least twenty-one other newspapers throughout the country published or elaborated on the new details from the Boulder police news conference. "The lack of concern about a killer on the loose" and "Patsy did not give DNA" was a headline in most of those newspapers. That included newspapers in California, Indiana, Wisconsin, Virginia, South Carolina, Texas, Ohio, Tennessee, Washington, Oregon,

Hawaii, Nevada, Idaho, and Indiana.

If the police investigators were trying to turn attention away from their initial bungled case by pinpointing Patsy and John Ramsey as suspects, it was working, judging from the headlines. Yet by leaking the wrong information, they were perpetuating their bungled case for those looking back on their actions.

> "The public is not in any danger." CBS News,
> December 31, 1996

> Wednesday, January 1, 1997
> John Ramsey Pilots His Plane to Funeral.
> "John Ramsey is a pilot and flew the family to Georgia in his plane." *Rocky Mountain News* January 1, 1997

The Daily News in New York republished the information. "**John Ramsey, head of a $1 billion computer company and amateur pilot, was allowed to fly his own plane to Atlanta, where his daughter was buried yesterday.**"

The story was false. Two pilots from John Ramsey's company flew the family to Atlanta for JonBenét's funeral and then back again to Boulder after the funeral. John Ramsey was told about the erroneous article weeks later and reacted with: "I couldn't have flown a plane. I could barely walk or function. I was so broken with grief." The Ramsey family was never contacted before the story was published. The story was never publicly corrected, and eight months later, the inaccurate information was used in a major magazine article.

"Speculation can really screw up an investigation," says the homicide expert. "And the reporter didn't second source the information."

Thursday, January 2, 1997 Boulder Mayor statements:
No signs of forced entry into the home.
No killer on the loose.

Boulder Mayor Leslie Durgin blasted her opinion to the *Boulder Daily Camera,* the *Rocky Mountain News,* CNN, and others while continuing and reinforcing the statements from the Monday news conference. She stated, "It's not like there's someone walking around the streets of Boulder prepared to strangle young children." She was responding to a CNN interview Patsy and John Ramsey had done the night before, Wednesday night, January 1, 1997. In the interview, the Ramseys warned "There's a killer on the loose." The mayor was reiterating, emphasizing, and speculating without basis.

"We don't think there should be cause for undue concern"—Boulder Public Information Officer, NBC News January 2, 1997

Mayor Durgin also elaborated on the Ramsey case with a stunning remark about evidence. Boulder police reports prove she was wrong.

"There were 'no visible signs of forced entry in the house' where JonBenét was found dead," declared Durgin.

Actually, eight areas of possible and questionable entry were found in the Ramsey home and written about in police reports:

1. Fresh Pry Marks: "Solarium door (facing south): fresh pry mark damage near the dead bolt appeared to be two or three separate and distinct areas of attack. The 'missing wood chips' were not

located in the vicinity of the door." (BPD Report #1-59) (The solarium door is in the southeast corner of the home.)

"Ms. [name redacted], a neighbor, stated that the only suspicious thing that she observed was that the inside of the Ramsey residence in the southeast corner room, the light was not on. This was suspicious for the light in that room has been on continuously for the last few years." (BPD Report #1-98)

2. Unlocked Window: "Living room: three-paned window. a wreath covered the middle pane, which was unlocked but closed. An extension cord ran between the window and its frame and led to the outside." (BPD Report #1-59)

3. Unlocked Window: "Formal dining room: the middle panes of the eastern- and western-most windows were both closed, but unlocked. Statue and flower arrangements were in front of these windows, which prevented the windows from being opened." (BPD Report #1-59)

4. Open Door: "French door along the west wall: no signs of forced entry to the door, which was ajar." (BPD Report #1-59)

5. Pry Marks: "South rear residence door northwest of the grate: the exterior screen door appeared to have damage in the area of the handle lock consistent with the door being forced open with the lock engaged. It looked like the force supplied to the lock mechanism came from the inside out. No pry marks on the exterior." (BPD Report #1-59)

6. Open Door Butler Pantry: Interviews with two witnesses state the door was open: When John's friend arrived at the Ramsey home at 6:01 a.m., he "found the butler kitchen door standing open about one foot while it was still dark outside and before the evidence

team or Det. Arndt arrived." (BPD Reports #1-1490, #1-1315)

At 8 a.m., a neighbor whose home was just to the north of the Ramsey home "got up and observed a basement door leading into a kitchen area was standing wide open." (BPD Report #1-100 Source)

The second listed witness was referring to the butler kitchen door.

7. Smudged Window Frame: "Northeast basement bath: two areas on the bottom frame were clear of dust. The impressions were consistent with the application of fingers to the area. The associated area inside the residence showed smudge marks on both walls above and just south of the toilet. A piece of garland similar to that found in the wine cellar (storage area where the child's body was found) was found stuck to the wall in the east impression." (BPD Report #1-59) "A partial shoe impression was found on the top of the toilet cover in the northeast basement bathroom." (BPD Report #1-59)

8. Metal Grate Disturbance Area: "Metal grate: below the broken basement window direction under the grate were observed leaves and other exterior debris." (BPD Report #1-61) Further examination of the metal grate evidence area showed a suitcase under the broken west-facing basement window. This was shown in the first video Boulder police took of the crime scene. It was speculated a suspect used it as a possible way out of the home. The suitcase contained clothing and a toy belonging to JonBenét. It was not her suitcase.

Boulder police crime scene photograph showing suitcase below open window and scrape on the wall in the basement of the Ramsey home. It's a possible entry point into the home. Photo taken on December 26, 1996.

Further examination of the metal grate disturbance area showed Homicide Detective Lou Smit easily able to climb through a metal grate, through a broken basement window, and into the basement of the home.

Homicide Detective Lou Smit was hired in March of 1997 by the Boulder district attorney to give an outside perspective on the botched JonBenét Ramsey murder case and determine if he could help salvage the case. Smit is demonstrating in these two photos (see also next page) how easy it is to climb through the window well and into the basement. He is proving his theory that this is a viable point of entry for an intruder.

None of the information about possible ways into the Ramsey home was released to the public, including the possible "forced entry" at the south solarium door, the northeast basement bath, and the metal grated window well. Reporters who covered the case are still surprised to learn about it because they didn't know until now that there was evidence of forced entry into the home.

Friday, January 3, 1997 Mayor holds National News Conference
> **No forced entry into the house.**
> **No killer on the loose.**
> **Not a random act.**

Mayor Durgin held forth to the nation and parts of the world by countering Patsy and John Ramsey's Wednesday night CNN interview with her own publicity campaign. In her CNN televised news conference, she reiterated her beliefs that there was "No killer on the loose." There was "No forced entry into the house." This was "Not a random act."

Boulder Police Chief Tom Koby publicly supports the mayor's comments.

"People have no reason to fear." Mayor Durgin, CBS News, January 3, 1997
> **"No evidence of a break in." ABC News, January 3, 1997**

John Temple was managing editor of the *Rocky Mountain News* during the Ramsey murder. He spent more than fifteen years supervising coverage on the case. He was also managing editor for the *Washington Post.*

"We talk about trust in our society, trust in our institutions, trust in media. When you break that trust and then it's discovered, the ramifications are extremely serious. In a case like this, it means we don't trust law enforcement. It's very disturbing to trace the information released. Their deliberate behavior utilizing inaccuracy to prove their points is so wrong."

> **Saturday, January 4, 1997**
> **No forced entry.**
> **No killer on the loose.**

ABC News, CBS News, NBC News, *The Daily News* in New York, *The Sacramento Bee, Albuquerque Journal,* and the Twin Falls, Idaho *Times-News* all quoted portions of the mayor's news conference from the day (Friday) before. "Not a random act," "No visible signs of forced entry," "No need to fear someone wandering the streets." All were elaborated on and all were quoted as coming from the mayor of Boulder. The media and the public relied on the mayor as knowing fact, when in this case, it was actually fiction.

> **"No killer lurking in the streets . . . unusual."**
> **"No evidence the house was broken into."**
> **"No sign of forced entry." CNN News, January 4, 1997**

"Call me naïve, but I am still shocked when an officer speaks as a public servant, and they lie," says John Temple.

"There is no excuse for lying from public figures. It is a dereliction of their duty. It is a corruption that is a cancer for the public trust," says Frank Scandale, *Denver Post* metro editor during the initial JonBenét coverage and currently director of investigation for the *Journal News* as part of *USA Today* in New York. He has first-hand experience with Ramsey case coverage, as does John Temple. Both were newspaper managers when JonBenét was killed. Neither knew the lying by Boulder police and the district attorney was this widespread.

The mayor told me in an interview after her comments, "I was not consulting the police chief." In a later interview for a 1999 documentary that aired in the United States and Britain, she disputed and contradicted her own statement, saying she regularly consulted the police chief and specifically cleared her statement that there was "not a killer on the loose" with him. We're including what she said.

> *The Case of JonBenét—The Ramseys vs. the Media*
> **Mayor Leslie Durgin: It was done in large part to allay the fears of the children in our community and to let people know that the information that I had at the time was that we did not have some crazed person on the streets of University Hill.**
> **Interviewer: And who did you clear it with?**
> **Mayor Leslie Durgin: The police chief.**

Those who were following the case closely through media reports, including other media, were successfully led into the "Ramseys Did It" viewpoint through this daily barrage of untrue information.

"They framed us for murder. It was a calculated move on their part. It has continued for twenty-five years," says John Andrew Ramsey, John Ramsey's son from his first marriage. He has the benefit of hindsight and twenty-five years of being part of the family suspected of killing JonBenét. He was in college at the University of Colorado when his half-sister was murdered.

That was just the first week of coverage in the JonBenét Ramsey case.

CHAPTER 4:

PUBLICITY—ONGOING

The onslaught of untruths and inaccuracies continued without pause after that first week of daily falsehoods. In the months ahead, leaks to the media persisted and were deliberately incorrect. The campaign to focus attention away from the disastrous investigation and to convince people the "Ramseys Did It" was succeeding.

The Ramsey story was reported for sixteen consecutive days on all of the four then-dominant national evening newscasts: ABC, CBS, CNN, and NBC. It was significant, and in most cases, damning publicity. Video of JonBenét Ramsey performing in beauty pageants began appearing on Monday, December 30, four days after her body was discovered. Photographers who attended the pageants sold their video and still pictures to a willing media where it was read and watched by an eager public.

January 19, 1997—"JonBenét Gets Hair Colored." *Newsweek Magazine*

Radio and television talk shows had their new topic for the week—"What kind of mother does this to a six-year-old child?"

It wasn't true. But it launched another unpleasant myth about Jon-Benét and her family, that her hair was dyed blond.

Patsy and John Ramsey said it wasn't true, family members and friends stated JonBenét's hair was not colored. Further research shows that very blond hair like JonBenét's ran in the family, specifically with pictures of John Andrew Ramsey and John Ramsey as children, both with white-blond hair.

The article strengthened the inference that it was Patsy Ramsey (bad mother) who killed JonBenét. No reliable hair salon was found that claimed to dye JonBenét's hair to its blond color.

The information was republished in several newspapers including in this article nine months later: **"JonBenét's hair is dyed white-blond, her lashes are curled and her lips are brushed a bright red."** *Denver Post,* October 12, 1997.

February 27, 1997—Incest Suspicions

Former Miss America Marilyn Van Derbur Atler of Denver was crowned Miss America in 1958. After her win and after her father died, Van Derbur Atler said she was a victim of incest. So, this next leak and what came with it were particularly cruel, mean, and not true.

"Ex-Miss America Interviewed Twice in Ramsey Investigation." Boulder Daily Camera, February 27, 1997

The article examined Atler's history as an "outspoken victim of incest" and detailed her work for child abuse and incest survivors.

Following the exclusive and leaked story to the *Boulder Daily Camera,* television, radio, and other newspapers interviewed Atler. She spoke frankly about her interviews with Ramsey case investigators and their discussions about her experience with incest.

Ninety-three newspapers throughout the country published the story, and the *CBS Evening News* broadcast it, relying on Atler and the

Boulder Daily Camera for information.

John Ramsey's daughter had been brutally tortured and killed. Now, police and the district attorney interview a known incest survivor about her experiences and then leak the fact that they questioned her about incest to the media.

Law enforcement knew JonBenét was not a victim of incest. They'd had time to absorb the reports of JonBenét's pediatrician, the coroner who performed the autopsy, and another doctor from Children's Hospital that the coroner brought in for a portion of the autopsy. All three, experts in their areas, said JonBenét showed "no prior signs of abuse of any kind." Their opinions were available to police after the autopsy was performed and two weeks later, from a letter by the pediatrician. This is one of many examples where Boulder police investigators and the Boulder district attorney ignored inconvenient evidence (no prior abuse), in favor of their own opinions (incest).

"It's an example of why strong leadership on the case was needed to shut people up and have one line of communication," says the homicide detective. "Too many people were involved and influencing the case. Somebody has an idea that they think this is what it is—incest— and says, 'We don't believe those supposed expert doctors. They don't know what they're talking about.' In spite of that thinking, they were allowed to investigate and leak."

JonBenét's pediatrician would have lost his medical license if he thought she was being abused and didn't report it to authorities during the time he treated her. The State of Colorado statute for mandatory reporting by physicians of physical or sexual abuse was adopted in 1969.

Francesco G. Beuf, M.D., FAAP
2880 Folsom, Suite 100
Boulder, CO 80304
(303) 442-2913
Caring for Infants, Children, and Teenagers

January 18, 1997

My office treated JonBenet Ramsey from March, 1993, through
December, 1996. Throughout this period, there has been
absolutely no evidence of abuse of any kind.

Francesco Beuf, M.D.

JonBenét's pediatrician wrote this letter for Ramsey case investigators with Boulder police on January 18, 1997. It was written more than a month before the leak by the Boulder District Attorney's Office and resulting article alleging incest in the Ramsey case. The case investigators from the district attorney's office and the police department would have known the incest allegations were untrue based on expert analysis.

Patsy Ramsey Wrote the Ransom Note

In the weeks following JonBenét's murder, both John and Patsy Ramsey rewrote the ransom note several times for police using both their left and right hands. The note was initially analyzed by the handwriting expert from the Colorado Bureau of Investigation. Their analyst asked for five handwriting tests from Patsy Ramsey.

Ultimately, six handwriting experts were brought in to examine the note. Two were hired by the Ramseys' defense attorneys. Boulder police hired three more and included the CBI analyst so there were a total of four handwriting examiners asked for comment by Boulder police.

John didn't write the note, they determined. Patsy, who was most often leaked as the writer of the ransom note, most likely didn't write it, according to the experts who judged her on a scale of one to five. All six experts, from prosecution and defense, decided she was within one point of "not being the ransom note writer." The Secret Service handwriting expert, whose agency is the international expert in counterfeiting and handwriting, gave a definite opinion to Boulder police who had asked for it: Patsy Ramsey did *not* write the ransom note, the agent wrote in his analysis. According to reports and leaks to the media, Boulder case investigators wouldn't accept that. They believed Patsy wrote the ransom note. They had already been leaking for months and continued to do so.

"Ransom note author likely was Female, Sources Say"
—*Boulder Daily Camera*, March 8, 1997
"Ramsey Probe Focuses on Mother's Handwriting"
—*Colorado Springs Gazette*, March, 1997

"Handwriting Points to Patsy Ramsey Sources Say. Sample Contains Characters with Some Features seen in Ransom Note"—*Rocky Mountain News*, March 19, 1997

"ABC News has learned . . . There are similarities between handwriting of Patsy Ramsey and the ransom note. There is not enough to prove conclusively that Patsy Ramsey wrote the note."—ABC News, March 19, 1997

Homicide expert perspective: "Handwriting is an OK investigative discipline. It's not DNA, not fingerprints, and it's not serology. It's a tool."

March 11, 1997—"No Footprints in Snow Means No Intruder"—*Rocky Mountain News*

"Snow at Ramsey House Lacked Footprints. Absence of tracks among First Clues that led Police to Suspect Members of Family."—*Rocky Mountain News*

The information came from two police sources, according to the reporter on the story. The reporter did not contact the Ramsey attorneys for a possible explanation or fact check.

It was false information.

Crime scene photographs from the morning JonBenét went missing show there is no snow on the south side of the home.

These are Boulder police crime scene photos from the morning of December 26, 1996. The photos show no snow on the south side of the Ramsey home. This directly contradicts the police leak expressing concern about no footprints in the snow. They would have been aware of these photos when they leaked the false information on "no footprints in the snow."

The pictures of no snow on the sidewalks and south-facing patios were convincing and made the false story even more outrageous.

The story was also countered in the written reports from the second officer to arrive on the scene the morning JonBenét was reported missing: "Sgt. Paul Reichenbach does not believe there was snow on the sidewalks or on the driveway." (BPD Report #5-3916)

In a Boulder Police Department Affidavit for a Search Warrant from March 1997, Sgt. Reichenbach again deals with the condition of the yard and noted in his report "that there was a very light dusting of snow and frost on the exposed grass in the yard outside the Ramsey home. Some of the grass and yard was covered with snow from previous snowfalls and this snow was described as being crusty and measuring one-two inches deep. Sgt. Reichenbach states that he saw no fresh footprints in any of the snow or in the frost on the grass."

The false story was published in forty-four newspapers throughout the country on March 11, 1997, and eighteen more newspapers published it the next day on March 12.

Newspapers from thirty-eight states published the story. The primary story was "No footprints in the snow led police to suspect the Ramseys." But the other story line also utilized by most of these newspapers was that there were "No signs of forced entry." The "no signs of forced entry" story first surfaced on January 2, 1997. It had a long and continuing life.

If the reason for the leak was to once again vilify the Ramseys, it worked. It took years for the information to be corrected. Some still believe it to be accurate.

September 16, 1997—*Vanity Fair* Errors

Peering through splayed fingers

Too smart to write a ransom note that long

John pilots his jet to his daughter's funeral

JonBenét was redressed

Normal-sized person couldn't get into basement
window

John Ramsey loses temper about money

John Ramsey hires attorneys

Ramseys get all copies of "most sensitive critical police
reports"

Ligatures on JonBenét's neck were "very loose"
consistent with staging

John Ramsey's children arrive at 7:55 p.m.

Patsy Ramsey's handwriting set off alarm bells

The inside information in Boulder that summer of 1997 was that a *Vanity Fair* reporter, Ann Louise Bardach, was in town to get the "real" story on the JonBenét case. Several officers on the Ramsey case stepped right up to put their spin on their part in the beleaguered case, especially after the incompetent first day of the police investigation.

Highlights from the article were repeated in 228 newspapers across the United States, Australia, and England.

"Peering at him through splayed fingers held over her eyes"
The first responding officer on the Ramsey crime scene was Officer

Rick French. He didn't talk to *Vanity Fair* about why he didn't find JonBenét's body in the basement cellar of the home. But French or someone else did remember something to tell *Vanity Fair* that wasn't in his police report or even in follow-up formal debriefings with his supervisors about that morning. Patsy Ramsey, the *Vanity Fair* article said, was watching French while "peering at him through splayed fingers held over her eyes." The inference that was repeated in newspapers throughout the country from the *Vanity Fair* report was that Patsy Ramsey was more concerned about police response than she was about her missing daughter.

Officer French didn't mention the "splayed fingers" aspect of Patsy's behavior in his police report or even when he was interviewed by supervisors, and he does contradict the *Vanity Fair* story in his police report, writing that he "thinks the Ramseys are acting appropriately."

And in his formal interview and debriefing on January 10, 1997, French makes several statements about the parents and their grief.

"John Ramsey would break down and start sobbing." (BPD Report #5-3839)

"Every time the phone rings, Patsy stands up and just like takes a baseball bat to the gut and then gets down on her knees and she's hiding her head and crying as soon as that phone rings and it's like a cattle prod." (BPD Report #5-3859)

The police report and interview weren't public. The *Vanity Fair* article was. And, all across the universe, ultimately, Patsy Ramsey was "peering (at a police officer) through splayed fingers held over her eyes."

"He (Hunter) wondered aloud whether 'Someone as smart as Ramsey would write such a long note'"

Boulder District Attorney Alex Hunter evidently thought it was appropriate to wonder aloud to *Vanity Fair,* while he was leading an active homicide investigation, whether "someone as smart as Ramsey would write such a long (ransom) note." DA Hunter also referred to John Ramsey as an "ice man" in the magazine article.

How is it appropriate for the district attorney to theorize about John Ramsey's behavior during an active and ongoing murder case that he's supposed to be in charge of?

District Attorney Hunter was speculating on his suspicions when he didn't have the evidence. It's a violation of the Rules of Professional Conduct for an attorney, especially a district attorney. He was not asked to respond before the Colorado Bar Association, but his public guesswork did have repercussions. In 1998, Governor Roy Romer effectively removed Hunter from most decision-making on the upcoming Ramsey grand jury. Further, what effect would Hunter's public conjecture have on a trial?

John Ramsey pilots jet to Atlanta

The *Vanity Fair* article repeated the claim that John Ramsey flew his jet to Atlanta. **"On December 29, the family flew to Marietta, Georgia, in a private jet, piloted by John Ramsey, for JonBenét's funeral."**

That incorrect information was taken from a headline in the *Rocky Mountain News* eight months earlier that wasn't retracted. And it wasn't true. The family was flown to Atlanta and back to Boulder by two pilots in a plane from the company that John Ramsey headed up.

"JonBenét was redressed."

Evidence including clothing traces left on her bed dispute that statement. JonBenét was not redressed.

"No one but a small child or a midget could have crawled through that space" (metal grate basement window area).

Homicide Detective Lou Smit proved this was untrue when he crawled through the metal grate basement window.

"She's gonna spend every last penny I make." (John about Patsy)

Wasn't true. John Ramsey said, when asked, that this was untrue. He added, "There was always enough money. Money was certainly not something to get angry about at this time in our lives."

John Ramsey hires attorneys.

Untrue. John's business attorney made the decision to hire attorneys for the family. John didn't know about the decision until he was told later they had attorneys. He said he was "incapable" at the time of making that kind of decision. The *Vanity Fair* article stated, "Ramsey decided that his wife should have her own lawyers, and he retained Patrick Burke and Patrick Furman."

"Ramseys have been provided with copies of all 'the most sensitive and critical police and detective reports.'"

This again is untrue. The Ramsey family received a copy of the ransom note from Detective Linda Arndt, unsolicited by the family, and without prior approval of the Boulder Police Department in

December. Writer and reporter Ann Louise Bardach mentioned that fact but only later in her article. On April 21, 1997, the Ramsey attorneys received thirty-two pages of police report copies from first responders relating only to what happened the morning of December 26, 1996. The police reports were in exchange for agreed-upon interrogations with Patsy and John Ramsey scheduled for April 30, 1997. By then, there were hundreds of other police reports that the Ramseys and their attorneys did not get. *Vanity Fair* writer Bardach followed up with: "They (Ramsey attorneys) held fast to their demand for a copy of the entire police file." Untrue. Ramsey attorney Hal Haddon said, "We never asked for the entire file. That's unrealistic and not something we would expect." They got what they asked for—thirty-two pages of first responder police reports.

"The ligatures around her neck (and right wrist) were, investigators say, 'very loose' consistent with staging."

This is untrue. The coroner in the autopsy report describes a white cord around her neck: "Wrapped around the neck with a double knot in the midline of the posterior neck is a length of white cord similar to that described as being tied around the right wrist." The coroner then spends a full paragraph in the autopsy writing about the damage to JonBenét's neck, noting that a "deep ligature furrow encircles the entire neck." Autopsy photographs show the rope embedded around her neck. The report was publicly released in August of 1997, weeks before the article was published and with enough time to be used for fact-checking. The autopsy date of release was also mentioned in the *Vanity Fair* article. The Boulder officers who were supplying the information to the *Vanity Fair* reporter would know the story wasn't true based on the

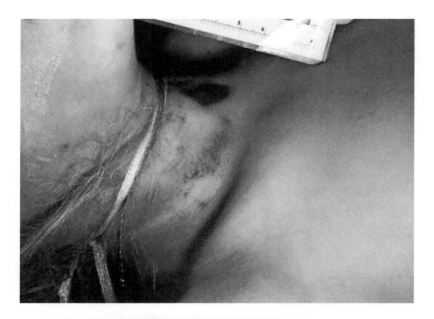

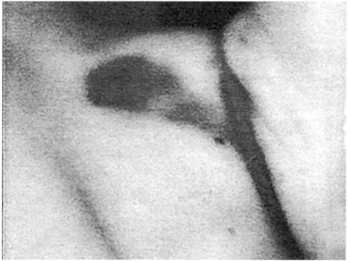

The rope was tied so tightly around JonBenét's neck that it left a "furrow" (as described by the coroner) from the ligature/rope. It completely encircles her neck. The two autopsy photos show the rope that her body was found with and the furrow once the rope is removed.

autopsy and on autopsy photographs of the child's neck. Investigators had access to both the autopsy and photos shortly after the murder and months before the *Vanity Fair* article in September 1997.

"John Ramsey's children arrived at the Ramsey house at 7:55 p.m."

This is wrong. It refers to the time John's children, John Andrew and Melinda, arrived at the Ramsey home after traveling from Minneapolis and Atlanta where they spent Christmas. They arrived at 1:30 p.m., in time to meet John and Patsy at the family home after JonBenét's body was found and with time to travel with the family to a friend's home where they were staying.

"'Out of the 74 names submitted for testing, Patsy's handwriting was the only one that set off alarm bells,' says an investigator closely tied with the testing of the ransom note."

Here it is again. As just discussed earlier in this chapter, this is still not true. More than half of the handwriting analyzed by others was not ruled out. In spite of evidence discounting that Patsy wrote the note, there were police leakers who simply ignored and would not accept that evidence. They continued to leak their erroneous mantra that Patsy wrote the ransom note. Evidence from the six handwriting analysts consulted by Boulder police and the Ramsey attorneys said she didn't write the note or probably didn't.

The reporter and writer of the *Vanity Fair* article, Ann Louise Bardach, stated to me when I questioned the errors: "No one compared to the level of fact-checking that we did." The *Vanity Fair* article was devastating with the number of errors it contained.

"(Ransom note) Written to mislead and written by a woman"—CBS News, September 7, 1997

More than 230 newspapers, plus some television networks, published or broadcast stories about the *Vanity Fair* article.[3] A large number of the articles were pre-coverage promotion of what the September 16 *Vanity Fair* article would report. The pre-coverage promotion articles were published on September 4, 5, 6, and 7 of 1997. They focused on what the magazine told them would be in the article—that Patsy was the suspect as the ransom note writer.

The articles that were published after that magazine article included information quoted from the magazine. The information circulated worldwide, including an article from Sydney, Australia.

The Ramsey attorneys were outraged and demanded an investigation from Boulder Police Chief Tom Koby. Chief Koby responded by demanding polygraphs of the primary detectives on the case to find out who leaked to reporter Bardach. Those polygraphs never happened. Instead, Chief Koby backed down and sent a letter to the Ramsey attorneys three days later stating there was no evidence the Boulder Police Department had authorized or condoned any improper releases of information. The Boulder City Manager sent a letter the same day as the police chief to one of the Ramsey attorneys saying the city "will not investigate" to find the sources of the *Vanity Fair* article.

What chance did any of us have for honest information and an unbiased and objective look at the Ramsey case investigation? All of the following headlines are false or lack evidence.

Monday, December 30, 1996
>No DNA from Patsy
>No Danger from a Killer on the Loose

Tuesday, December 31, 1996
>No DNA from Patsy
>No Danger from a Killer on the Loose

Wednesday, January 1, 1997
>John Ramsey Pilots His Plane to Funeral

Thursday, January 2, 1997 Boulder Mayor statements:
>No signs of forced entry into the house
>No Killer on the Loose

Friday, January 3, 1997
>Mayor holds National News Conference
>No forced entry into the House
>No Killer on the Loose
>No Random Act

Saturday, January 4, 1997
>No forced entry into the House
>No Killer on the Loose
>No Random Act

January 19, 1997
>JonBenét gets her hair colored

February 27, 1997

Incest suspicions

March 11, 1997

No Footprints in Snow Means no Intruder

September 16, 1997 *Vanity Fair*

Patsy peering at him (officer) through splayed fingers held over her eyes

DA Hunter wondered aloud whether someone as smart as Ramsey would write such a long note

On December 29, the family flew to Marietta, Georgia, in a private jet, piloted by John Ramsey, for JonBenét's funeral

JonBenét was redressed

No one but a small child or a midget could have crawled through that space (metal grate basement window area)

She's gonna spend every last penny I make

Ramsey decided that his wife should have her own lawyers, and he retained Patrick Burke and Patrick Furman

Ramseys have been provided with copies of all "the most sensitive and critical police and detective reports"

The ligatures around her neck (and right wrist) were, investigators say, "very loose" consistent with staging

John Ramsey's children arrived at the Ramsey house at 7:55 p.m.

Patsy Ramsey's handwriting set off alarm bells

John Temple, who was managing editor at the *Rocky Mountain News* during this period, believes, "It takes time for the truth to emerge especially when the first message is the most remembered. The investigators were dishonest and incompetent and some media didn't have appropriate standards. In the frenzy of this chaotic investigation, the police got away with it for a long time."

How and why did they do it? Why did police officers, detectives, and top management with Boulder police allow and actively participate in deliberate misinformation and incorrect leaks? It starts at the beginning of the case where the decision on guilt was made.

When the group of Boulder officers, the chief, detectives, and FBI agents were told JonBenét's body had been found, they were gathered at the police department and had been there for three hours determining what they should be doing about what they thought was a missing and kidnapped child. They should have been at the crime scene, which was the Ramsey home.

The news that her body had been discovered came with a realization that they should have found it hours earlier, when they first searched the home. One of the officers in that meeting told me that thought hit him with an incredible impact. He was sickened, both by the fact that they hadn't located her and that she was dead.

It was then, according to that officer, that another Boulder officer in the meeting said angrily in a lowered tone, "I knew it. They killed their daughter."

And that's when it began.

The belief that Patsy and John Ramsey were guilty was immediate. Members of the department, who were just beginning to understand how badly they had botched the investigation, reacted by setting a course that is still difficult to comprehend or grasp. They believed that everything was fair in their attempt to recoup their reputations and solve the case. That included shading and abandoning the truth to help them however it could.

That these false information releases, and then leaks, happened is devastating. That it became an immediate priority in the investigation is unimaginably ruthless and unfair for the people whose lives it affected.

An officer who was involved in the investigation early on explained to me recently why the false information and leaks happened. "They were on this crusade to avenge JonBenét's death while destroying the family. I've never seen cops act this way. It is still hard to believe. It was the end justifies the means beyond any reasoning. Whoever came up with it, an FBI agent or the officers themselves, doesn't matter. What matters is they made it their mission."

The homicide detective explains further about why he believes Boulder police were dishonest with leaks and news releases. "You've got this agency that's north of the big city, Denver, and the attitude is that we're going to show them we can handle these big cases. What they should have been doing was seriously investigating the case with experienced people and following protocol. Yet they rejected all immediate offers of help from Denver police and Aurora police. They weren't getting help from the more experienced jurisdictions because they didn't think they needed to. So you have lack of experience, poor management, inferiority complex type stuff. They needed to do 'all' of it right, and they never did."

CHAPTER 5:

EVIDENCE

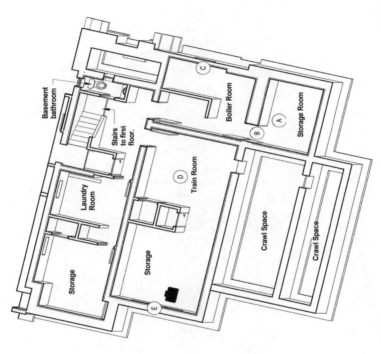

Ramsey Basement

A   JonBenét's body.
B   door opens outward.
C   Exposed ventilation duct.
D   Train room.
E   Broken window and suitcase.

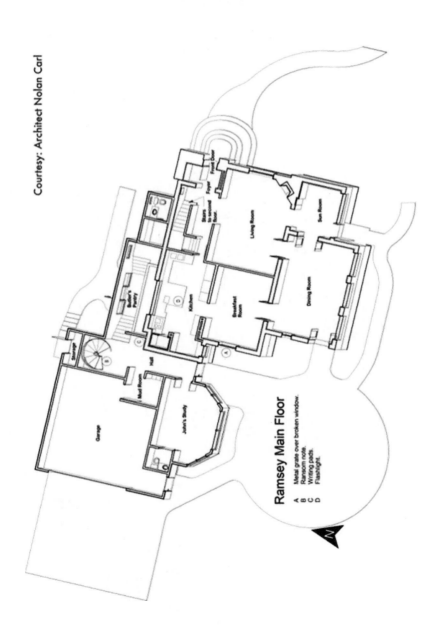

Courtesy: Architect Nolan Carl

Ramsey Main Floor

A   Metal grate over broken window.
B   Ransom note.
C   Writing pads.
D   Flashlight.

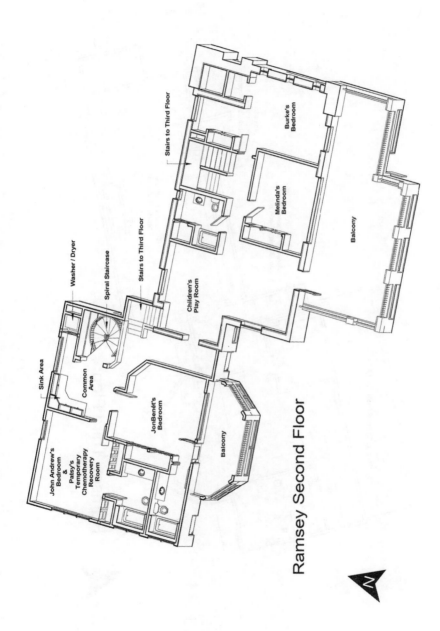

Ramsey Second Floor

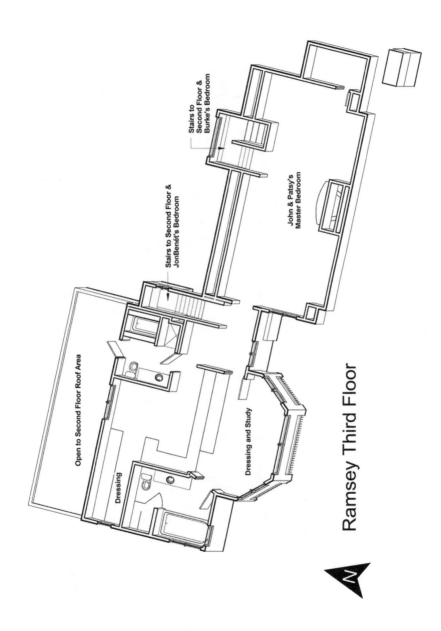

Stairs to
Second Floor &
Burke's Bedroom

Stairs to Second Floor &
JonBenét's Bedroom

John & Patsy's
Master Bedroom

Open to Second Floor Roof Area

Dressing and Study

Dressing

Ramsey Third Floor

N

If you're inside a home where a crime has occurred, you're it. You're a suspect.

A necessary part of a twenty-five-year look at the JonBenét Ramsey murder is to examine evidence accumulated in the case, which I also did in my first book. The evidence hasn't changed much over twenty-five years. What it means has.

"There's an old saying in law enforcement and that is the first witness is the first suspect. There is occasionally a connection between the people who reported the crime and the people who committed the crime," the homicide detective I consulted says and adds. "There are two reasons to look at the family in the home first. If they are responsible, you need to handle the scene appropriately. If they are not responsible you need to take the steps necessary to eliminate them and find new suspects. That's what a defense attorney is going to do."

There has always been confusion as to what the evidence was for or against on JonBenét's murder, mostly because of the mistakes made and the indecision that prevailed. Here is some of what was considered evidence in the Ramsey case and perspective on its importance.[4] The three most critically important pieces of evidence were JonBenét's body, the ransom note, and DNA. The size of the Ramsey home was certainly a factor and indicated the killer had to have some knowledge of the residence. All of the evidence should be considered as possibilities for the prosecution or the defense in a criminal trial.

SIZE OF RAMSEY HOME

To truly understand the size of the home and the relationships of the various areas to each other, I've included 3D drawings of the Ramsey home from the basement, the main floor, the second floor, and the third floor. I've marked the areas of specific interest on each floor. There were four floors used in the home. The home had 104 windows; 100 of them opened to the outside. There were a variety of window and door locks in the home.[5] There were seven doors on the main floor that opened to the outside. The Ramseys had an alarm, but it wasn't active on the night JonBenét was murdered. In fact, they rarely used it, both parents said.

JonBenét's body was found in the Ramsey basement, as designated on the drawing. The stairs leading to the basement are nearly straight down the hall from the storage room. They are stairs the killer used. That basement storage room was also referred to as the wine cellar, something the family jokingly called it before JonBenét's body was left there. The room was never a wine cellar. It was originally used for coal storage when the home was built in 1927. The interior was roughed-out concrete.

JonBenét's bedroom was on the second floor on the west end of the home. There are three other bedrooms on that floor, including her brother Burke's bedroom on the opposite or east end. There's also a large playroom, and two balconies. You can see in the drawing the spiral staircase leading from the main floor to the second floor that ends near JonBenét's bedroom. The stairs to the third floor also start near JonBenét's bedroom. John and Patsy's bedroom was on the third floor of the home. I have also included photographs of both staircases.

Stairs from Patsy and John's third floor master bedroom to the second floor ending next to JonBenét's bedroom.

Spiral staircase leading from second floor next to JonBenét's room to main floor next to kitchen. The ransom note was left on the third step from bottom on the spiral staircase.

The master or main bedroom was created in the third-floor attic space as part of an extensive remodel the Ramseys did. There are two sets of stairs leading to and from the third floor. One set ends close to JonBenét's bedroom. Another set of stairs on the other end of the master bedroom leads from the third floor to the main floor of the home. Those stairs go near Burke's bedroom on the second floor. Patsy and John's bed was nearer Burke's room than JonBenét's room on placement in their bedroom.

The home had an elevator when the Ramseys bought it, which was removed as part of their remodel. The home measured 7,000 square feet when it was sold after the murder. The drawings underscore the complexity and size of the home. Whoever killed JonBenét had to have some familiarity with the home. Possibilities include a family member; an outsider who had been in the home secretly several times; someone who had walked through the home when it was open to the public for Christmas tours; someone on the years-long remodeling crew; or a family friend.

JonBenét was put in bed at 9 p.m. on Christmas Day night. Patsy made the 911 phone call at 5:52 a.m. the next morning. That gives a narrow window for the killing and could indicate a lack of fear of discovery by the killer.

JONBENÉT AUTOPSY

The autopsy was performed on JonBenét the day after her body was found on Thursday, December 26, 1996. A day later, on Friday, December 27, seven people were present when the autopsy began. Two were from the Boulder Police Department, two were from the Boulder

District Attorney's Office, two were medical assistants, and the coroner was Dr. John Meyer. Dr. Meyer was trained as a forensic coroner, which means he had training in determining cause of death in violent and unexpected circumstances.

The autopsy gave a clear indication of what did and didn't happen when JonBenét was murdered.

The cause of death listed two reasons for her death: asphyxia by strangulation associated with craniocerebral trauma. Simply put, she was killed by strangulation and a blow to the head. In an interview with me Dr. Meyer said, "They are as close as happening simultaneously as I've seen. Enough so that I didn't know which happened first and listed them together as that's the most accurate."

The causes of death ruled out the convenient theories initially floated and leaked to main-stream media and entertainment talk shows. One of the most popular theories was that Patsy killed JonBenét because she was angry at her for bed wetting and hit her in the head or slammed her head into something hard enough for it to cave in a portion of her skull. That was the pet theory of one of the investigators on the case who leaked it freely to those who would listen. But there was no evidence that JonBenét had wet her bed, even though her underwear was urine-stained. To the contrary, the sheets on her bed were dry. They hadn't been changed because the sheets contained fibers from the clothing she had on that night and hadn't worn before. Additionally, the autopsy states the strangulation and blow to the head were simultaneous. The speculation that Patsy killed JonBenét with the blow to the head and then strangled her later as part of a cover-up was just that—speculation. Evidence showed the murder couldn't have happened that way. The strangulation and blow to the head were nearly "simultaneous," according to the coroner who told me that in an interview.

More detail in the autopsy opened the possibility that a stun gun was used on JonBenét for torture or control. That theory was investigated after marks on her body were noted in the autopsy report. A Colorado Bureau of Investigation officer believed it was possible. "Sue Ketchum of the CBI (Colorado Bureau of Investigation) is shown the photos of the marks and she indicated they could very well be made from a stun gun." (BPD Report #26-58) Homicide Detective Lou Smit, hired by the Boulder DA for his expertise, strongly believed a stun gun was used to subdue JonBenét. Boulder police rejected that idea. Acceptance of a stun gun being used also makes an intruder more likely. Here's what the autopsy says about those possible stun gun marks on her back: "On the left lateral aspect of the lower back . . . are two dried rust-colored to slightly purple abrasions." Similar abrasions were found on her lower right cheek.

Smit believed they were stun marks and spent extensive time researching. He found that the marks on her cheek and on her lower back matched one stun gun in use that left marks with the exact spacing that was left on JonBenét's body. Coroner Meyer had no experience with stun gun marks. Arapahoe County Coroner Michael Dobersen, was considered an expert and testified nationally about stun gun marks on bodies in violent crimes. He had done extensive testing on stun gun marks.

Dr. Dobersen believed the marks were probably from a stun gun. Detective Smit was convinced a stun gun was used. Dr. Meyer would not confirm. There was never a concrete resolution, but the information would have been introduced at a trial.

Before the autopsy was completed, Dr. Meyer asked a pediatric expert from Children's Hospital in Denver to consult on whether JonBenét had experienced prior sexual abuse. Dr Meyer had already determined from the evidence on her body that she had no prior sexual abuse. But he was ensuring that his decision was right by getting a second opinion. Dr. Andrew Sirotnik from Children's Hospital in Denver met Coroner Meyer at the morgue in Boulder. Both confirmed JonBenét Ramsey had not been sexually abused in the months leading up to the killing.

Remember, the date of the autopsy was December 27. That's when "no prior sexual abuse" was established by the coroner, a pediatric specialist he called in to assist, and JonBenét's pediatrician. In spite of that, almost two months later as I've discussed, the Boulder District Attorney's

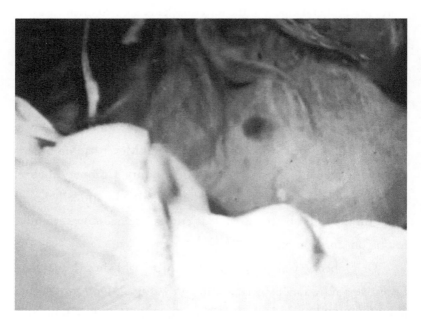

Possible stun gun mark on JonBenét's cheek.

Office and Police Department floated the leaked incest theory.

AMOUNT OF RANSOM NOTE RANSOM
AND JOHN RAMSEY'S BONUS

The ransom note asked for $118,000. The amount of John Ramsey's bonus was $118,117.50 that year. Not the same, but very close, and enough to trigger concern and raise the question: Who knew the amount of John Ramsey's bonus?

"It's certainly a connection. It's an interesting amount, an odd amount. Circumstantial evidence is considered real when there's a connection. There is one here and it's good circumstantial evidence, but it doesn't stand on its own. It can't be your only evidence." (Homicide expert perspective.)

Information about the ransom note demand and John Ramsey's bonus that year was provided to police by Ramsey defense attorney investigators. It was promptly leaked to the media who declared they were the same:

"Dead Girl's Dad Received $118,000 Pay for 1995. Same Amount Sought in Ransom Note."—*Rocky Mountain News*, January 22, 1997

"Year-end Bonus was $118,000."—NBC News, January 27, 1997

SIGNS OF FORCED ENTRY

There were several signs of forced entry into the Ramsey home including fresh pry marks on a main floor door, unlocked windows, unlocked doors, open doors, a smudged windowsill, and a metal grate disturbance from a main floor window well into the basement of the home.

BLANKET AROUND JONBENÉT

John Ramsey, who found the body, was questioned as to whether the blanket around JonBenét was wrapped loosely or tightly. Initially, he wasn't sure. The inference was if the blanket was wrapped tightly, then someone was trying to take care of her. The assumption was, therefore, one or both of her parents were involved.

"The fact that there is a blanket at all is a concern to me, not whether it's wrapped tightly or loosely. Why cover her with a blanket, instead of just dumping her? You're leaving more evidence with that blanket. The motive for that has to be considered, but more important is what evidence is left behind on the blanket." (Homicide expert analysis of the "blanket" evidence.)

PATSY RAMSEY WORE THE SAME OUTFIT THAT MORNING AS THE NIGHT BEFORE

"That's a so what. She's wearing the same outfit. So what?" (Homicide expert perspective.)

This was another leak to the media in the ongoing campaign to discredit the Ramseys. Entertainment shows touted detective beliefs that Patsy Ramsey hadn't had time to change her clothes that night because she was killing her daughter and covering it up.

NO SIMILAR CRIME BEFORE OR AFTER
JONBENÉT'S MURDER

"This could be a one-time crime because it was such a disaster, and those who did it would say, we're not going to do it again. And I look at the kidnapping of Charles Lindbergh's baby for a criminal history before this murder. (The Lindbergh kidnapping in 1932 was a huge case, given the incredible popularity of Charles Lindbergh, the first person to fly across the Atlantic.) There was no predicate for Lindbergh. There was nothing similar before the kidnapping of his baby. It can be something or it might not be." (Homicide expert perspective.)

Several months after JonBenét was murdered, in September of 1997, an intruder broke into the second floor of a home in Boulder. He sexually assaulted a fourteen-year-old girl. He was interrupted when her mother heard something and came into the room. The suspect, in a ski mask, fled and jumped out the second-floor window. Of note: He had broken into a home to attack the teenager when her mother was in the home and sleeping on the second floor. Detectives from the Ramsey case investigated, but were unable to find a suspect.

THE RAMSEYS DIDN'T ACT RIGHT

"What does that mean? How are grieving parents supposed to act and did these investigators have the experience to be able to judge?" The homicide expert is critical of that theory.

The "Ramseys didn't act right" theory was another leak to the media. Detective Linda Arndt, who turned her police report in thirteen days after JonBenét was killed, said in her report that John Ramsey

JonBenet Ramsey
Civilians/Items

EMOTIONS

Per previous high school teacher - Patricia was very distraut at the funeral [1-557]

Patsy cries all the time [1-640]

Per Det. Arndt, on the morning of December 26, 1996 Patsy's facial expression and look in her eyes was that of someone who appeared to be confused or dazed. [1-746]

AMR personnel quickly realized Ms. Ramsey was distraught [1-1121]

Lucinda Johnson [John's first wife] stated "John was devastated (at the death of his first daughter) and he is again." "He loved his daughters. He's a wonderful father and truly loves his daughters." #5-5

Per Melinda Ramsey - Patsy has really been in a state of shock. [5-209]

Per Melinda Ramsey answering the question, How is Burke reacting? She stated "I think in the beginning, you know he cried" [5-211]

During the initial ransom demand time Patsy was hysterical, just absolutely hysterical [5-230]

Per a family friend - During the initial contact he had during the ransom demand he stated that John Ramsey was not only visibly distressed he was absolutely just the pain that John was feeling was just palpable. I could feel it. This was John in a way I've never seen him before. He was absolutely at the end of his rope. He just put his head in his hands and cried and shook, you know. [5-234]

Per Jeff Ramsey - He (John Ramsey) was devastated. I mean he was crying and praying [5-278]

John was devastated. He carried her upstairs from the basement and near the time of the funeral he still acted like he was holding her in his arms and would just fall to pieces. [5-352]

She is hyperventilating. She is hallucinating. She is screaming. She was hysterical. John was pacing around. Their friends were trying to keep Patsy from fainting. She was vomiting a little. [5-404]

Patsy was literally in shock. Vomiting, hyperventilating. (This during the ransom time) [5-433]

I thought Patsy was going to have a heart attack and die. I thought she was going to kill herself. [5-437]

Patsy on the floor hysterical [5-446]

When John Ramsey finds the body he screams [5-464]

John Ramsey was clearly in a lot of pain. (Friend) [5-473]

Patsy was hysterical holding a crucifix [5-484]

These summaries of Boulder Police Reports are filed under *Emotions*. They have never been published. The report summaries reveal the Ramseys' emotions during the ransom wait, and after JonBenét's body was found. They contradict reports that the "Ramseys weren't acting right." [The punctuation used is verbatim from the Murder Book Summaries].

"smiled, joked" while she was talking with him that Thursday morning. John Ramsey denies it. Detective Arndt's report is suspect. Homicide reports should be turned in within twenty-four to forty-eight hours of the investigator's observations otherwise they are considered "recall" reports and very rarely accepted by district attorneys in more experienced jurisdictions. Boulder investigator comments in at least three police reports contradict the "didn't act right" portrayal. They note that several times the family is grief-stricken and having a hard time functioning. Police investigators with the family for their first night after the murder observe both parents are sobbing through most of the night. Police reporting of the first responders in their reports and also in their debriefings note the family is very emotionally grief-stricken. A summary of some of the police reports of John and Patsy's emotions is attached.

A CHILD'S SCREAM THAT NIGHT

A neighbor who lived across the street and one house south of the Ramsey home "was awoken by what she described as one loud incredible scream, obviously from a child, that lasted three to five seconds and stopped abruptly, and the scream sounded like it had come from across the street south of the Ramsey residence." (BPD Report #1-175)

Why then, didn't John, Patsy, or Burke hear or react to the scream if that's what happened? Detective Smit found that the scream could have come from the Ramsey basement through an exposed ventilation duct which was open to the outside. He conducted tests and found that a scream could be heard outside of the home but not inside the home on the third floor. His tests were conducted using the open ventilation duct. The vent is marked on the 3D basement drawing of the home and is close to the basement storage room where JonBenét's body was found.

PAINTBRUSH, ATTORNEYS, AUDIO FROM 911 CALL

Other concerns expressed by police case investigators: the paintbrush portion used for the garrote came from Patsy's paint brush, the family hired attorneys which indicated guilt, and audio from the 911 call indicates Burke was recorded at the end of it when his parents say he was still in bed asleep.

The 911 call audio information has been discredited numerous times as not reliable because audio testing doesn't detect Burke's voice on the end of that emergency call. That scenario has been dropped from the case.

The paintbrush being used in the garrote was spun to cast guilt on the Ramseys, who were depicted as using a garrote after a fatal blow to the head as a last-minute device to cover up their daughter's murder. But the coroner's determination of two nearly simultaneous causes of death rules this particular theory out. The fact that a portion of Patsy's paintbrush was used to fashion the garrote is considered "of interest," but not necessarily for whom.

The Ramseys say friends hired attorneys to protect them only after it was determined that police had suspected them of killing JonBenét almost immediately. John told me initially in an interview that he was too grief-stricken to consider something like hiring attorneys at that early date and didn't comprehend that attorneys had been hired for him and Patsy.

"Broken Brush in Ramsey's Art Supplies, Source says.
Stick used in JonBenét Slaying described in autopsy report."
—*Rocky Mountain News*, September 5, 1997

HI-TEC BOOT PRINT FOUND NEAR JONBENÉT'S BODY

An imprint from the Hi-Tec brand of work boot was found in the basement storage room in mold near where JonBenét's body was found. (BPD Report #1-1576, BPD Report #1-1594)

This is a crime scene picture of a Hi-Tec boot print left in mold next to JonBenét's body. It was never traced to anyone known to be in the Ramsey home.

There was an extensive examination of all the Ramsey's footwear, including those in their extended family. No Hi-Tec boot was found. All the investigators who were in the home, including crime scene personnel, were questioned about what they were wearing during their examination of the home. Additionally, those involved in the remodel of the home, as well as the Ramsey's housekeeper and her husband, were questioned and sometimes searched. No Hi-Tec connection was found.

OTHER EVIDENCE POSSIBILITIES

There is other physical evidence that could indicate an intruder, including:

- Partial shoe imprints were found near JonBenét's body and on the toilet tank cover in the basement of the northeast bathroom. (BPD Report #1-1518) It did not trace to the Ramseys or any investigators.

- An unidentified pubic hair was found on the white blanket partially covering JonBenét's body. (BPD Reports #1-1440, #3-128) It did not trace to the Ramseys or any investigators.

- There was also a scuff or drag mark under the open basement window where the suitcase was located. There was glass and debris from outside on top of the suitcase. (BPD Reports #1-65, #1-101, #1-90, #5-421)

- The suitcase under the window contained a pillow sham, a duvet, and a Dr. Seuss book. All belonged to the Ramseys. The suitcase was not used regularly by any of the Ramseys. It was suggested that the items were "comfort" items for JonBenét. (SMF146, *Wolf vs. Ramsey* deposition.)

- JonBenét's body had been wiped off, but no liquid was found. Investigators thought she'd been wiped off to disguise and destroy any DNA left on her body.

- Small pieces of material from a brown paper sack containing a rope and found underneath John Andrew's bed did not belong to the Ramseys and fibers from it were found in JonBenét's bed.

- There are at least twelve items used in the murder that are missing from the home including the rest of the duct tape, the rest of the rope used to strangle her, and a possible stun gun.

What does it mean? Our homicide expert says it was initially a relatively simple case of a missing child, but with the missing child protocols not being followed, the Boulder police case investigators ultimately missed a lot in a bungled investigation. "On this case, you have to consider the original investigation and factor it into the evidence that was there and the evidence that was missing. Their searching wasn't done well. They didn't find the child's body when they searched the home. Was the missing evidence simply not recognized as evidence either by the case investigators or by the eighteen friends and family in the home that morning, including John and Patsy?

"There is a lot here that just doesn't make sense. There are a lot of puzzling things. Evidence doesn't support that it's the Ramseys, any more than it supports that someone came in from the outside. There's a lot of physical evidence about John and Patsy Ramsey, but they live there. The investigation was done so poorly that many of the things that are now questioned, there are no answers for. These are mistakes you can't recover from."

Ultimately, he believes:

"They have a lot of circumstantial evidence, but in today's world, this is the kind of case that a district attorney is going to look at and they're going to want to get much more than they have. They don't have a convincing case."

CHAPTER 6:

EVIDENCE—
THE RANSOM NOTE

Mr. Ramsey,

Listen carefully! We are a group of individuals that represent a small foreign faction. We ~~do~~ respect your bussiness but not the country that it serves. At this time we have your daughter in our posession. She is safe and unharmed and if you want her to see 1997, you must follow our instructions to the letter.

You will withdraw $118,000.00 from your account. $100,000 will be in $100 bills and the remaining $18,000 in $20 bills. Make sure that you bring an adequate size attache to the bank. When you get home you will put the money in a brown paper bag. I will call you between 8 and 10 am tomorrow to instruct you on delivery. The delivery will be exhausting so I advise you to be rested. If we monitor you getting the money early, we might call you early to arrange an earlier delivery of the

This is a copy of the two-and-a-half-page ransom note that Patsy Ramsey said was left on a step on the spiral staircase in the home.

money and hence a earlier
~~delivery~~ pick-up of your daughter.
Any deviation of my instructions
will result in the immediate
execution of your daughter. You
will also be denied her remains
for proper burial. The two
gentlemen watching over your daughter
do not particularly like you so I
advise you not to provoke them.
Speaking to anyone about your
situation, such as Police, F.B.I., etc.,
will result in your daughter being
beheaded. If we catch you talking
to a stray dog, she dies. If you
alert bank authorities, she dies.
If the money is in any way
marked or tampered with, she
dies. You will be scanned for
electronic devices and if any are
found, she dies. You can try to
deceive us but be warned that
we are familiar with Law enforcement
countermeasures and tactics. You
stand a 99% chance of killing
your daughter if you try to out
smart us. Follow our instructions

and you stand a 100% chance
of getting her back. You and
your family are under constant
scrutiny as well as the authorities.
Don't try to grow a brain
John. You are not the only
fat cat around so don't think
that killing will be difficult.
Don't underestimate us John.
Use that good southern common
sense of yours. It is up to
you now John!

Victory!
S.B.T.C

These are the words of the person who killed JonBenét. At the very least, they are the words of someone who allowed it to happen.

The ransom note was two-and-a-half-pages long. Patsy said she found it on the third step from the bottom of the spiral staircase that curled into the kitchen of the Ramsey home. Patsy told police officers: "Whoever left the note knew I always came down those staircases in the morning." (BPD Report #5-403)

It is 372 words in length and written in block print. Whoever wrote the note used a black Sharpie felt-tip pen like one found in the Ramsey home. The Secret Service compared the ink and found it was the "same type of ink as was on the ransom note." So what was found and tested was the pen used to write the ransom note or it was another similar one.

The tablet that was used was found in the Ramsey home. There were others in the home like it. These tablets were checked by police because their paper matched that of the ransom note and they were in plain view in the kitchen. The particular tablet used for the note was found by matching tear marks at the top of the page in the tablet with tears at the top of the ransom note.

John and especially Patsy were note writers and used tablets frequently, according to what they told police. If a killer had taken a tablet outside the home, it most likely wouldn't be missed.

A partial greeting, "Mr. and Mrs. /" was also found in the tablet and deemed a "practice note." Several pages that were torn out of the tablet, based on tear marks, were never found.

"Most investigations follow Occam's razor (a scientific and philo-sophical rule)—that the simplest explanation is the most correct. Why would someone take a chance of writing the note in the house and start out with a practice note unless they had to. If you were an outsider and knew you were going to leave the note, why not have that prepared, set it down, and get in and get out. You wouldn't need a practice note. You have to consider those questions about the practice note." (Homicide expert perspective.)

It is an oddly detached, somewhat rambling note. There seems to be no real anger even though it threatens "your daughter being beheaded"—a terrible and tormenting thought for the parents of a missing child—and several times threatens "she dies." There is no profanity, and there are words not commonly used like "attaché" and "fat cat." And curiously, JonBenét's name was not mentioned in the note. Explanations for that include the killer didn't know her name or didn't know how to spell it, or that person was deliberately disassociating from JonBenét.

The questions always asked about the note include whether it was written for a real kidnapping gone wrong or as a cover up. That hasn't been determined and won't be until and if a killer is caught and explains.

The note seems to taunt. It could be an "I am smarter than you" lesson. Does the note seem somewhat immature? If it seems immature or juvenile, does that mean it's written by someone in their twenties, as opposed to someone older?

One consideration is whether the note used phrases or ideas from several movies. If some of the ransom note phrasing came from movies, then the writer would have had to watch the movies to collect the quotes. Translation: premeditation.

"Don't try to grow a brain, John" could come from the movie *Speed,* released in 1994. In that movie, the killer says, "Do not attempt to grow a brain."

Other possibilities are these crime movies compared for phrases used in the ransom note: *Dirty Harry, Ruthless People, Nick of Time,* and *Ransom.* All were released before JonBenét's murder. Three of the movies center on kidnapping, one focuses on an extortionist, and the other is about a serial killer.

None of the movies were found in the Ramsey home. The Ramseys did not go out for movies. The movies they did have were for children. The movie theory came from Homicide Detective Steve Ainsworth, who was on loan from the Boulder Sheriff's Department, and Homicide Detective Lou Smit. They started looking after Detective Ainsworth remembered similar phrasing in the movie *Dirty Harry.*

Here's something to note: Four of the five movies listed use words and phrasing such as "listen," "listen up," "now listen to me carefully," "now listen," and "listen very carefully."

The main text of the ransom note after the greeting starts with "Listen Carefully" when it would make more sense to say, "Read Carefully," instead of "Listen."

This line in the Ramsey ransom note: "If we catch you talking to a stray dog, she dies," was considered by Ainsworth and Smit as possibly prompted by this sentence from *Dirty Harry:* "If you talk to anyone, I don't care if it's a Pekingese pissing against a lamp post, the girl dies."

Or from the movie *Nick of Time:* "You talk to a cop, you even look at a cop too long and your daughter's dead . . . I'll kill her myself. Cut the head off right in front of you." Does this suggest similarities to this sentence in the Ramsey ransom note: "Speaking to anyone about your situation, such as Police, F.B.I., etc., will result in your daughter being beheaded."

The movie *Ransom* uses the wording "We have your son." The Ramsey ransom note uses "We have your daughter."

Overall, the movies are a possible explanation for some rather odd suggestions and wording in the note. Accepting the possibility that words and ideas from movies were used for ransom note writing meant embracing the possibility of an intruder. Boulder police investigators rejected the movie idea.

There was a lot of speculation about the closing of the Ramsey note:

Victory!
S.B.T.C.

There were several theories for what the initials represent. None are accepted as valid because no one really knows.

The ransom note doesn't make sense, except to the killer who left it. Why was it left in the home? What was its purpose? How does one make sense of something so bizarre and depraved?

The note remains incredibly intriguing as well as brutal. It's been a compelling part of the mystery of the Ramsey case for twenty-five years and was one of the initial pieces of the case that has enthralled and captivated so many people for those twenty-five years.

The reality is that the answers to the unending questions on the Ramsey ransom note come down to this: Nothing will be answered until the killer chooses to tell us.

CHAPTER 7:

EVIDENCE—DNA

"This case can be solved," says a consultant who was brought in on the Ramsey case in the early years of the investigation. "It can be solved in two ways." And for the first time in a long while, we find there is something new about the Ramsey case and more than one differing opinion about whether the case can be solved.

"The first way is if someone knows and acknowledges the few pieces of information on the case that have been withheld. Very few people know that there is information that hasn't been released. The second way the case can be solved is if the remaining DNA is submitted for testing for family or genetic DNA and a match is found."

The consultant adds, "Most of us are familiar with the numbers of cold cases that have been solved nationwide using genetic DNA. The Boulder police Ramsey case investigators have to decide to use the remaining DNA for those purposes. It's a hard decision when so little DNA is left. They will most likely use all that remains. But why would they save it? What does that accomplish?"

One answer might be waiting for newer DNA technology, which is evolving constantly and dramatically, and allows for smaller amounts of DNA to be used for profiling, according to DNA experts I consulted. Some believe waiting for more and unknown DNA breakthroughs may make sense for the case. Others believe the DNA should be tested now for genetic comparison purposes.

Genetic DNA offers real and serious possibilities in solving cold cases. DNA from crime scenes is compared to DNA on ancestry websites to see if there's a biological or family relationship. Millions of people in search of their ancestors routinely submit their DNA to ancestry websites. It is genetic information that subscribers voluntarily make public. Investigators compare their crime scene DNA to the ancestry sites to find certain genetic similarities. When they find those, they trace back through families to find a probable suspect in the family tree.

That's how thirty-four-year-old Sylvia Quayle's killer was caught. Sylvia was described by friends as a "good and kind person. Always ready to help out." In August of 1981, someone broke into her home in Cherry Hills Village, Colorado. Sylvia was attacked, sexually assaulted, and was found dead by her father on August 4.

It was a well-publicized case in part because of where Sylvia was attacked and murdered. Cherry Hills Village is a wealthy and secluded area in the metropolitan area of Denver. It has very little crime. There was the perception that people were very safe there. There was great unease and concern about her death.

Nearly forty years after she was murdered, Sylvia's killer was arrested. DNA advances allowed for new testing on DNA left behind at the scene, which weren't feasible or even known about in 1981. Investigators developed a DNA profile and entered it into two separate family DNA websites. They found similarities to one family and traced back into family history to find a relative and probable suspect in that existing family tree. Eventually the investigators were able to get a DNA sample from the suspect by examining his garbage. Crime scene DNA matched what was found on a coke can from his garbage. A sixty-two-year-old man from Nebraska was arrested and charged with Sylvia's murder.

The Golden State Killer was found using DNA genetic profiling. He was a former police officer in California and on no one's radar as a suspect in the deaths of at least thirteen people, the rapes of fifty others, and a hundred and twenty burglaries over thirteen years. Joseph DeAngelo was found after investigators first created a profile using genetic material from the rape kit of one of his victims. They tried one well-known ancestry site and then another. The second ancestry site identified a relative who was close to the suspect's genetic sample. Then investigators traced other relatives in that family to find their most likely suspect, Joseph DeAngelo. He pleaded guilty before going to trial to avoid the death penalty. He is serving twenty-six life sentences in a California prison.

There are two officers from the Boulder Police Department currently in charge of the Ramsey case. The two were on the original case in 1996, twenty-five long years ago. They will be involved in making the decision on whether the remaining Ramsey DNA should be used to try to find a killer by searching genetic DNA.

The two Boulder officers are Detective Commander Tom Trujillo and Special Services Commander Ron Gosage.

According to information in the Ramsey Police Report Summary files, Trujillo was involved in the Ramsey case that first day and in the home that night on the day JonBenét's body was found. The other officer still on the Ramsey case, Ron Gosage, joined the case on Saturday, December 28, 1996, and initially assisted during DNA testing of the Ramsey family that day.

They won't discuss the case because it is still considered an active cold case. They say their hours on the case vary depending on tips and what they describe as "other work." They say they work at least weekly on the case.

They are the only original case investigators still with the Boulder Police Department. There are questions from those with and outside law enforcement as to whether both of these officers should still be on the case given their predisposition to believe Patsy Ramsey killed her daughter.

Trujillo is listed as the investigator on the DNA report prepared for the Colorado Bureau of Investigation on December 30, 1996. On that report, Trujillo lists the offense as: Homicide—Willful Kill—Family. The Suspects listed are: Patsy Ramsey and John Ramsey. Investigators on the case had determined and vocalized from the first day that John and Patsy were their primary suspects.

```
                  COLORADO BUREAU OF INVESTIGATION
                         LABORATORY REPORT

    LAB CASE NUMBER:D96-4153   SECTION:DNA TESTING
    AGENCY NAME: C00070100 - PD BOULDER
    OFFENSE: 0902 - HOMICIDE - WILLFUL KILL-FAMILY
    INVESTIGATED BY: DET. THOMAS TRUJILLO          SUBMISSION DATE: 123096
    * SUSPECT(S):                    AKA:/                 R/S   D.O.B:
      RAMSEY,PATSY                                         W/F
      RAMSEY,JOHN                                          W/M

    * VICTIM(S):
      RAMSEY,JONBENET                                      W/F

          Kathren M. Brown Dressel
    EXAMINED BY/ KATHREN M. BROWN DRESSEL, LABORATORY AGENT/CRIMINALIST
    DATE COMPLETED/JANUARY 15, 1997
```

Detective Tom Trujillo, who as of June 2021, is in charge of the Ramsey cold case, submitted this request for testing to the Colorado Bureau of Investigation. It is dated December 30, 1996. The offense is: Homicide–Willful Kill—Family. The suspect(s) are: Ramsey, Patsy and Ramsey, John. Twenty-five years ago, the document states Trujillo's belief that Patsy and John murdered their daughter.

Neither Gosage nor Trujillo had homicide experience when they were assigned to the Ramsey case.

As of the updating of this chapter in June of 2021, Gosage and Trujillo and their supervisors, including the Boulder police chief and the Boulder district attorney, have decided not to use the remaining Ramsey DNA for genetic testing to try to find a killer.

There are three known tests on the DNA taken from JonBenét's body and that remaining DNA is what was used by the Colorado Bureau of Investigation and Cellmark Labs.

The first test was concluded in January 15, 1997, and was from underneath fingernails of each hand and from blood in her panties. The DNA was mixed with blood. The Colorado Bureau of Investigation did the testing. That DNA test result excluded John, Patsy, and Burke Ramsey and other family members and friends. It showed a mix of DNA from JonBenét and from another person who has been referred to as Unknown Male #1.

An aside: In the controversy of the chaotic investigation, Boulder police made the decision to not share the results of that first DNA test with the Boulder district attorney. Both were the law enforcement agencies involved in the case, supposed to be working together, and involved in trying to solve the case. That decision underscores the poor relationship between the two law enforcement entities that continued and was inherited by the next district attorney and caused more dysfunction in trying to find JonBenét Ramsey's killer.

The results of that first DNA test—which excluded John, Patsy, and Burke Ramsey—were not leaked to the media and were not shared publicly.

COLORADO BUREAU OF INVESTIGATION
LABORATORY REPORT

LAB CASE NUMBER:D96-4153 SECTION:DNA TESTING

AGENCY NAME: CO0070100 - PD BOULDER

OFFENSE: 0902 - HOMICIDE - WILLFUL KILL-FAMILY

INVESTIGATED BY: DET. THOMAS TRUJILLO   SUBMISSION DATE: 123096

* SUSPECT(S):   AKA: R/S   D.O.B:
  RAMSEY, PATSY   W/F
  RAMSEY, JOHN   W/M

* VICTIM(S):
  RAMSEY, JONBENET   W/F

EXAMINED BY/ KATHREN M. BROWN DRESSEL, LABORATORY AGENT/CRIMINALIST

DATE COMPLETED/JANUARY 15, 1997

EXHIBIT	DESCRIPTION
#5A, 5B	BLOODSTAINS FROM SHIRT.
#7	BLOODSTAINS FROM PANTIES.
#14B	BLOODSTAIN STANDARD FROM JONBENET RAMSEY.
#14I	SWAB WITH SALIVA.
#14L, 14M	RIGHT AND LEFT HAND FINGERNAILS FROM JONBENET RAMSEY.
#15A, 15B	SAMPLES FROM TAPE.
#16A	BLOODSTAIN FROM WHITE BLANKET.
#17A, 17C	BLOODSTAINS FROM NIGHTGOWN.
#23A, 23B	SEMEN STAINS FROM BLACK BLANKET.
#32B-2	BLOODSTAIN STANDARD FROM JOHN ANDREW RAMSEY.
#33B-2	BLOODSTAIN STANDARD FROM MELINDA RAMSEY.
#34B-2	BLOODSTAIN STANDARD FROM JOHN B. RAMSEY.
#35B-2	BLOODSTAIN STANDARD FROM PATRICIA RAMSEY.
#36B-2	BLOODSTAIN STANDARD FROM BURKE RAMSEY.
#42B-2	BLOODSTAIN STANDARD FROM
#43B-2	BLOODSTAIN STANDARD FROM
#44B-2	BLOODSTAIN STANDARD FROM JEFF RAMSEY.
#47B	BLOODSTAIN STANDARD FROM
#48B	BLOODSTAIN STANDARD FROM

RESULTS:

DEOXYRIBONUCLEIC ACID (DNA) PROFILES FOR THE LISTED GENETIC LOCI WERE
DEVELOPED FROM THE FOLLOWING EXHIBITS:

EXHIBIT #	DQA1	LDLR	GYPA	HBGG	D7S8	GC	D1S80
14B (JONBENET)	1.2,2	BB	AB	BB	AA	AC	INC
32B-2 (JOHN ANDREW)	1.2,3	BB	AA	AB	AA	BC	24,28
33B-2 (MELINDA)	1.2,3	BB	AA	AB	AB	BC	24,28
34B-2 (JOHN B.)	1.2,1.2	BB	AA	BB	AA	BC	24,28
35B-2 (PATRICIA)	2,3	BB	--	-			

CONFIDENTIAL

This is the first page of the Colorado Bureau of Investigation DNA report. It was submitted on December 30, 1996 and returned on January 15, of 1997. I have redacted names that are not Ramsey family names. None of the names submitted matched the DNA that was collected from JonBenét's body.

The second DNA test was at the request of Boulder police and was concluded in May of 1997. It was conducted by CellMark Labs in Maryland. It found similar results to the Colorado Bureau of Investigation testing. CellMark Labs also excluded John, Patsy, and Burke and showed a mix of DNA results from JonBenét and from another person.

In 2003, the Denver Police Department Lab prepared the Ramsey DNA for possible inclusion into CODIS. CODIS is a national data bank operated by the FBI. The data bank stores DNA from known convicted offenders. It also stores DNA from unknown offenders from criminal incidents. To be accepted into CODIS, DNA must have eight to thirteen specific identifiers known as alleles. It is a strict protocol and allows the FBI to maintain standards from qualified DNA. Even though the Ramsey DNA on the unknown male is considered weak, it had enough information to be admitted into CODIS.

The CODIS data bank is accessible to law enforcement. If a DNA profile matches what is in CODIS, the appropriate law enforcement is notified.

The third DNA test was conducted in 2008 by Bode Labs in Virginia. Mary Lacy, who was district attorney at the time, and whose background was in sexual assaults, asked for the lab to check in two previously untested areas of the long johns JonBenét was wearing when she was murdered. Lacy theorized a sexual predator would have pulled JonBenét's long johns and panties down to sexually assault her. Lacy asked for testing on the inside and outside of the waist band of the long johns on both sides and compared it to one site in JonBenét's underwear. The DNA found under JonBenét's fingernails from the 1997 DNA tests was not mentioned.

A new and advanced system of testing called "touch DNA" was

used. Bode Labs, which had tested and matched thousands of DNA cases throughout its history, found that the "touch DNA" submitted from previously untested areas on JonBenét's clothing *matched* the DNA from her body tested in 1997.

In a July 2, 2008, letter to John Ramsey, Lacy explained her findings and her decisions and concluded, "Despite substantial efforts over the years to identify the source of the DNA, there is no innocent explanation for its incriminating presence at three sites on these two different items of clothing that JonBenét was wearing at the time of her murder."

District Attorney Lacy exonerated the Ramseys of killing their daughter. It's a decision that was accepted with relief by some and widely decried by others, including the Boulder police investigators who continued to leak their displeasure and focus on one or both of the Ramseys as the killers of their daughter.

Recent examination of available documentation on the three DNA tests from outside experts questions whether there is one unknown male or two, which would result in a total of three DNA profiles in the samples being used and taken from JonBenét. Yet the established DNA with Unknown Male #1 is what is currently in CODIS for comparison.

The search for a match to the killer's DNA doesn't stop with the Boulder Police Department. Some family members of Homicide Detective Lou Smit are actively involved in trying to find a killer using DNA. Smit, as you might recall, was hired by the Boulder District Attorney's Office and approved by Boulder police for outside perspective.

He resigned in September of 1998 because he felt the Boulder investigation was going in the wrong direction toward the Ramsey family and the case wasn't being fully examined with experienced homicide detectives. Smit died of cancer in 2010.

Lou Smit left behind a list of names and items that he thought were important to the case, including people he thought could include JonBenét's killer. The list isn't for the faint-hearted. Some of the leads Smit tracked included people accused of cruelty to children, participating in snuff films, pedophilia, molestation, sexual assault and battery on children. The Smit team is now methodically going through that list, highlighting the most likely suspect, and collecting DNA from that individual. Sometimes they ask for the DNA. Sometimes they gather it surreptitiously.

The Smit team does not have the actual DNA sample from the Ramsey case. Boulder police have that. But once the family has collected a suspect's DNA, they forward it to an experienced national lab that has conducted thousands of DNA tests. The newly collected DNA is then compared to the profile of Unknown Male #1, whose profile was identified in the first test on January 15, 1997, from the Colorado Bureau of Investigation.

It is difficult and expensive work.[6] It takes dedication, which they have. More than a year ago, Cindy Marra, who is Lou Smit's daughter and a primary investigator on the Smit DNA team, says the family involvement has expanded. Marra's daughters began a podcast on the case. All are efforts to help the Ramsey family and to honor their father and his work on the case.

Why continue? Cindy Marra explains. "It was important to my dad. Members of our current team had such a close relationship to him. We want to continue his quest. His dying wish was that the case not be forgotten. We respect that. Our loyalty to our dad to stand in JonBenét's shoes and find her killer motivates us."

It's possible a suspect is not in the DNA that has been collected. There are suspects being looked at by private individuals as feasible because of their backgrounds and proximity during the murder.

That is another option for Boulder police investigators: to actively investigate the viable suspects they initially tested twenty-five years ago who were discounted for non-matching DNA.

There is substantial hope with the Ramsey family that the remaining mixture of DNA from their daughter and what they believe is her killer will be submitted by Boulder police for genetic comparisons. When or if case investigators determine they will ask for that testing or if they investigate suspects with non-matching DNA remains another part of the eternal mystery of the Ramsey case.

CHAPTER 8:

EVIDENCE—FAMILY HISTORY

John, Patsy, Burke, and JonBenét in family Christmas card portrait.

In the days following JonBenét's murder, Boulder police investigators began interviewing family, friends, professional acquaintances, neighbors, teachers, and anyone who knew the family. They interviewed people in Boulder, where the Ramseys lived, but also in Charlevoix, Michigan, where the Ramseys had spent summers for years, and in Atlanta, which was their hometown. The goal was to get the most accurate picture of what kind of people the Ramseys were and to see if there were any indications among those who knew them best that they murdered JonBenét.

What they found surprised some of them. Detective Steve Thomas, who believed Patsy killed her daughter, is quoted in one of those police reports. "It seems the theme that's being portrayed is this family John and Patsy were ideal parents, Christian people. It has been difficult at best during this investigation to uncover anyone that can offer any other perspective on the Ramsey's [sic]." (BPD Report #5-5026)

The reports centering on the background and history of the Ramseys covered eleven single-spaced pages in the Ramsey Murder Book Summary Index. I have redacted personal names in these reports for privacy reasons. I have also redacted incorrect information.

This is the first time these police report summaries have been made public. I have included all eleven pages of the summaries.

JONBENÉT RAMSEY MURDER BOOK SUMMARY INDEX

JonBenet Ramsey

Q

Civilians/Items

John Ramsey couldn't hurt anything or anybody (████████) [5-4613]

Relationship as a family is perfect. (████████) [5-4635]

If anything I wished my children were a courteous as Burke and JonBenet. (████████) [5-4639]

They hug each other. ....very very loving. (████████) [5-4659]

When I was around him, oh ..he was just crying and wailing and pacing the floor and breaking down with whomever he, you know, someone would hild him or whatever. He would just break down. (████) [5-4663]

████████....the nicest family you can ever be part of. An ideal family. [5-4683]

████████.....My general observation of Patsy and John as a family was that he was a high-powered business man that had tons oand tons of responsibility and he extremely loving and loyal to his family and spent all the time he had with his older children and younger children. And that they tried all the time to integrate and be together as one family with all the children, and that was the focus. [5-4723]

████████...Patsy who killed JonBenet. "(Patsy) I do not know" [5-4729]

████████...(when body brought upstairs), I think they were actu.. together,and their hands, they were together holding hands." [5-4735]

████████... (re: attorneys)...John said I have an attorney. ...I mean my recollection is that John was resistant to getting a lawyer [5-4736]

████████...and I know you won't but I mean I would lay my life on the line and tell you that no one in my family including Patsy, John or Burke has had anything to do with this. [5-4872]

████████...re: John Ramsey....whenever I've seen him areound the kids it's always been very gentle. Jon Benet gave him her medal. [5-4982]

Det. Thomas... it seems the theme that's being portrayed is this family John and Patsy were ideal parents, Christian people, it has been difficult at best during this investigation to uncover anyone that can offer any other perspective on the Ramsey's. [5-5026]

████████...I know that there was a lot of love in that family you know for the children. 5-5063...████████ was asked his opinion of any incest or inapropriate conduct and he replied ... Never, Never and That's the more incomprehensible to me. [5-5058]

████████...John Ramsey is generous, quiet caring...he always called the children. [5-5300]

████████.....Patsy was not obsessed with pageants. [5-5330]

████████...I never even heard Patsy raise her voice at either of the children. [5-5342]

████████...John was Crying, crying ah shaking, he was cold......Patsy was saying ....took my baby away. [5-5355]

6/03/98

JONBENÉT RAMSEY MURDER BOOK SUMMARY INDEX

There was a maid in the basement [1-97]

6/03/98

Per ▮▮▮▮▮▮ regarding JonBenet, "If she knew them she would have gone with them. If she didn't know them, I would assume she would fight like hell." [5-1425]

Per ▮▮▮▮▮: Q: "Have you ever seen John Ramsey angry?" A: "No." Q: "Did you ever see Patsy Ramsey angry?" A: "No." [5-1426]

Per ▮▮▮▮▮ the pilot for John Ramsey: He called the Ramsey house a few minutes after 6:00 a.m. and Patsy answered the phone and she was pretty hysterical. [5-1485]

The pilot ▮▮▮▮▮ stated that it was approximately 1:30 when he was called back and notified that JonBenet was dead. [5-1490]

According to ▮▮▮▮▮, " Burke just didn't know what was going on, I don't think." [5-1503]

According to ▮▮▮▮▮, ▮▮▮▮▮ may have made a statement to the Ramseys when he was fired, "You know I'm going to get you or bring you and your family down." or something like that. [5-1507]

Per ▮▮▮▮▮, JonBenet was so beautiful that many people would stop and ask if they could take her picture when she was walking down the street. [5-1628]

If JonBenet was abducted by a stranger she would have fought them like hell according to ▮▮▮▮▮. [5-1636]

Burke Ramsey once told ▮▮▮▮▮ "Aunt ▮▮, why are we hiding?" [5-1644]

According to Det. Steve Thomas he has not found any evidence of anger in regards to John Ramsey. [5-1742]

Per ▮▮▮▮▮, he overheard the comment at church, " Don't you just want to strangle her?" [5-1942]

John Ramsey is one of the most mild mannered guys, professional people I have ever met. [5-2542]

John Ramsey was very religious. [5-2549]

If you knocked on that door you couldn't hear anything because the bedroom -the master bedroom was 3 floors up. [5-2563]

You could feel love in their house. [5-2569]

per ▮▮▮ "but some sicko has gotten in there. [5-2571]

I am convinced wo ever did this murder, knew this house. (▮▮▮) [5-2572]

I believe they were much in love with each other. (▮▮▮) [5-2576]

It's just torn this family up. It shouldn't be like that, they don't deserve it. [5-2608]

Not excessive drinkers of alcohol. Never saw them spank the kids or anything. [5-2613]

Never seen John or Patsy angry. [5-2617]

6/03/98

JONBENÉT RAMSEY MURDER BOOK SUMMARY INDEX

JonBenet Ramsey

Civilians/Items

Officer French had probably 20 conversations with the Ramseys that were short and fragmented, there were distractions, and Officer French is getting bits and pieces. [5-3846]

Patsy describes JonBenet as going to bed with long underwear and a red top. [5-3846]

Det. Patterson had asked Ofc. French if there was any sign of break in and [French] told him no because he asked Mr. Ramsey if everything was locked and he said yes; is anything broken, he says no; and [French] accepted that but he does not know that for sure. [5-3852]

██████████...obviously two people in a lot of pain and not much was said. [5-4127]

John came in and joined her on the floor and there was just a lot of emotion, crying and so forth. It went on for quite a while. [5-4158]

John doesn't display anger, just being incredulous about who could have done such a thing. (██████████) [5-4161]

John's been described to us as a kind, caring, religious, family-oriented man. He is very quiet and reserved. [5-4201]

John very, verey seldom gets angry. [5-4437]

I never saw John lose his temper one time, I never saw him abusive. Very moral individual. [5-4448]

(██████████) "I have a very special relationship with the little girl". [5-4454]

Patsy was always so concerned about JonBenet (██████████). The girl was the consuming attention of the family. [5-4458]

"██ I think he's right. I think I need to make a statement." (John Ramsey to ██████████ after talking to ██████████". [5-4478]

██████████..."There's not a finer couple, two people who love their kids more than I've ever known in my life" [5-4481]

(██████████)..I don't hink he's mad at the Boulder Police, he just wants to find out whoever did this to his family". I've never seen 2 people grieve the way they have". [5-4482]

(██████████).. John phoned his children every night at eight [5-4534]

██████████.. "and I sad well, everybody hires attorneys. Everybody. [5-4544]

██████████....Patsy said Burke cried once. [5-4549]

John Ramsey never disciplined his children in his life. John would just pat them and love. [5-4550]

██████████...she told me that she had never seen JonBenet happier than Christmas day when she left her house. [5-4573]

John is a very focused person and a very dedicated family man. ██████ ██████. [5-4595]

6/03/98

JONBENÉT RAMSEY MURDER BOOK SUMMARY INDEX

JonBenet Ramsey

Civilians/Items

Patsy was a volunteer and a teachers dream. Donated $1,500.00 to the school music program. [5-3378]

Patsy was very gentle with JonBenet. [5-3383]

John would call his children all the time even in the middle of dinner. I never saw anything but gentleness. [5-3395]

At funeral Patsy angry "Wants answer" [5-3405]

(Patsy) they came in my house and took my baby. I have to go back. I have to know why. Why this happened.. I don't know who to trust back there. [5-3406]

John was a gentleman a super guy, a great guy. (▬▬) [5-3430]

▬▬...Burke had a great attitude he was always willing to participate. Great kid cooperative, funny. Really interacted well. [5-3439]

Patsy is really upset and afraid. [5-3467]

JonBenet would always be sitting with her dad. You know, she'd sit on his lap.

Mr. Ramsey was very caring with both JonBenet and ▬▬ my daughter.

JonBenet was very outgoing..was friendly and loved talking to adults. [5-3550]

John had gone to huge lengths to get her the best possible care, like flying her out to Maryland and seeing the best doctors there was. ▬▬[5-3560]

She(Patsy) was a very good mom toward the kids ▬▬, babysitter) [5-3608]

John didn't like JonBenet in the pageants. Patsy said she would take her out of the pageants if she didn't like them. [5-3609]

JonBenet and Burke were the most loving brother and sister I've ever seen. (babysitter,▬▬, Charlevoix) [5-3610]

(Ramsey per▬▬) Be totally cooperative with the police. (Was not badmouthing the police) [5-3675]

Per▬▬.....Saw nothing but a well adjusted family. [5-3681]

▬▬....I never saw any behavior from John that was even advancing toward a woman he was not the kind even the office to you know lay a hand on someon's arm or anything even those kinds of little things, I mean he did not have those behaviors, never. [5-3685]

Per▬▬ "John seldom gets angry". [5-3697]

Officer French does not know whether Patsy said that she went into get her daughter ready or whether she came down stairs first. [5-3837]

John Ramsey said all the doors were locked. [5-3840]

Patsy is the first to mention the FBI and asks police to check the airports. [5-3843]

6/03/98

JONBENÉT RAMSEY MURDER BOOK SUMMARY INDEX

JonBenet Ramsey

Civilians/Items

Mrs. ▮▮▮▮▮ stated that she heard one loud incredible scream and was the loudest most terrifying scream she had ever heard. It was obviously from a child and lasted from three to five seconds at which time it stopped abruptly. She thought surely the parents would hear that scream. The scream came from across the street south of the Ramsey residence. [1-175]

Regarding the Ramsey family per ▮▮▮▮▮▮ - "believes them to be the ideal family. Never a harsh or aggressive word or action." [1-180]

John Ramsey "I don't think he meant to kill her because she is wrapped in a blanket." Ramsey told them he had removed the tape from her mouth and unbound her hands. Patsy Ramsey pleaded for ▮▮▮▮▮ to bring JonBenet back to life. [1-182]

▮▮▮▮▮▮ stated that she has never seen any domestic problems between Patsy and John and that love was involved in the family as a whole. [1-202]

John was very dignified about his marriage. [1-208]

Stated that "I will share no privileged information." [1-212]

When told about JonBenet's death ▮▮▮▮▮ became quite upset and was crying. [1-227]

▮▮▮▮▮▮▮▮▮▮▮▮▮▮▮▮▮▮▮▮▮▮▮▮▮▮▮▮▮▮

▮▮▮▮▮▮, a friend of Patricia Ramsey, stated that Patricia Ramsey had dropped off a gift at their house at approximately 8:30 p.m. on Christmas [1-240]

John was doing a great deal of pacing and would frequently burst into tears while pacing. Neither one of the Ramsey's slept much that night and they were totally destraught. [1-240]

In conversation with Det. Arndt, Patsy Ramsey cried, her shoulders shook, and tears flowed from her eyes. This was during the interview regarding Burke Ramsey. [1-262]

"I hope you enjoy your daughter." (Supposedly stated by ▮▮▮▮▮ upon his dismissal.) [1-304]

According to ▮▮▮▮▮▮▮, "JonBenet would have fought her attacker." [1-328]

Richard Johnson described John Ramsey as being a person that loved his children and called the children every night at 7:30 pm. He was a good father, paid his bills and child support. [1-413]

According to ▮▮▮▮▮▮, JonBenet would have fought and kicked "I guarantee you." [1-447]

"Don't you just want to strangle her?" supposedly ▮▮▮▮▮ heard a voice behind him in church state this at a Christmas pageant at the church. [1-592]

The Ramsey's are a caring, loving family - per ▮▮▮▮▮. [1-616]

▮▮▮▮▮▮▮▮▮▮▮▮▮▮▮▮▮▮▮▮▮▮▮▮▮▮▮▮

JONBENÉT RAMSEY MURDER BOOK SUMMARY INDEX

JonBenet Ramsey

Civilians/Items

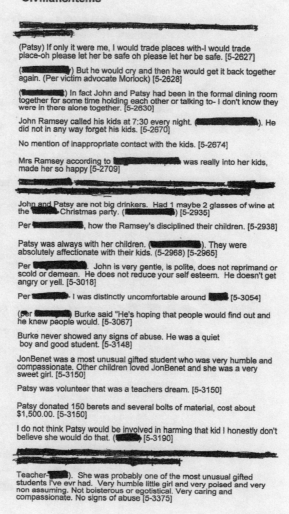

(Patsy) If only it were me, I would trade places with-I would trade place-oh please let her be safe oh please let her be safe. [5-2627]

(⬛⬛⬛⬛) But he would cry and then he would get it back together again. (Per victim advocate Morlock) [5-2628]

(⬛⬛⬛⬛) In fact John and Patsy had been in the formal dining room together for some time holding each other or talking to- I don't know they were in there alone together. [5-2630]

John Ramsey called his kids at 7:30 every night. (⬛⬛⬛⬛⬛). He did not in any way forget his kids. [5-2670]

No mention of inappropriate contact with the kids. [5-2674]

Mrs Ramsey according to ⬛⬛⬛⬛⬛ was really into her kids, made her so happy [5-2709]

John and Patsy are not big drinkers. Had 1 maybe 2 glasses of wine at the ⬛⬛Christmas party. (⬛⬛⬛⬛) [5-2935]

Per ⬛⬛⬛⬛, how the Ramsey's disciplined their children. [5-2938]

Patsy was always with her children. (⬛⬛⬛⬛). They were absolutely affectionate with their kids. (5-2968) [5-2965]

Per ⬛⬛⬛⬛. John is very gentle, is polite, does not reprimand or scold or demean. He does not reduce your self esteem. He doesn't get angry or yell. [5-3018]

Per ⬛⬛⬛⬛- I was distinctly uncomfortable around ⬛⬛⬛ [5-3054]

(per ⬛⬛⬛⬛) Burke said "He's hoping that people would find out and he knew people would. [5-3067]

Burke never showed any signs of abuse. He was a quiet boy and good student. [5-3148]

JonBenet was a most unusual gifted student who was very humble and compassionate. Other children loved JonBenet and she was a very sweet girl. [5-3150]

Patsy was volunteer that was a teachers dream. [5-3150]

Patsy donated 150 berets and several bolts of material, cost about $1,500.00. [5-3150]

I do not think Patsy would be involved in harming that kid I honestly don't believe she would do that. (⬛⬛⬛) [5-3190]

Teacher-⬛⬛⬛). She was probably one of the most unusual gifted students I've evr had. Very humble little girl and very poised and very non assuming. Not boisterous or egotistical. Very caring and compassionate. No signs of abuse [5-3375]

6/03/98

JONBENÉT RAMSEY MURDER BOOK SUMMARY INDEX

JonBenet Ramsey

Civilians/Items

Per ▮▮▮▮▮ - Patsy clearly is a religious person. [5-256]

Per ▮▮▮▮▮ - I think somebody came in the house and murdered her or somebody was actually trying to kidnap her for money. That was the motive in trying to get her out of the house. Got carried away or she tried to scream or something and then they had a body and what are they going to do. [5-257]

Per Patsy Ramsey to ▮▮▮▮▮ - "Somebody came to my house and murdered my baby." [5-296]

▮▮▮▮▮▮▮▮▮▮▮▮▮▮▮▮▮▮▮▮▮▮▮▮▮▮▮▮▮▮▮▮▮

He is a real family man with a stong professional drive - per ▮▮▮▮▮ [5-361]

Per ▮▮▮▮▮ - she stated Patsie and her were sitting in the Ramsey house at the time of the ransom and she was saying ▮▮▮▮ and then a couple of hour later we are looking at a dead girl. [5-387]

Patsy Ramsey's initial call to ▮▮▮▮▮, ▮▮▮▮ get over here as fast as you can. Something terrible has happened. [5-402]

Patsy told ▮▮▮▮▮ "All I know is she told me she didn't read the whole note." [5-403]

Whoever left the note knew I always came down those staircases in the morning. (Patsy Ramsey) [5-403]

▮▮▮▮▮ felt like he was a bad father compared to John Ramsey. He was unbelievably patient with his kids. Was really gentle with them and patient with them. Never heard him repremand either of them. [5-416]

Per ▮▮▮▮▮ - I was really frightened. I had a deep sense that her life was in danger and that she may be dead. I had an overwhelming feeling that she was in the house. [5-420]

Per ▮▮▮▮▮ - I have a gut feeling that who ever did this was very angry with Mr. Ramsey. [5-420]

"Why didn't Burke wake up when Patsy screamed?" [5-433]

Patsy was not upset over the bedwetting. [5-602]

Per ▮▮▮▮▮ - he sees these attorneys giving John bad advice. [5-711]

▮▮▮▮▮ stated "I never saw a bad bond in Patsy's body. You know she was just always so good." [5-982]

According to ▮▮▮▮▮ Patsy Ramsey was a vivacious, outgoing, honest with very high integrity and high morals. A loving and generous mother and friend. John is honest, strong, committed and caring. Extremely loving. [5-1011]

Per ▮▮▮▮▮ - that housekeeper is a liar. The housekeeper said at least three times about JonBenet getting kidnapped. [5-1042]

JonBenet would fight - per ▮▮▮▮▮. [5-1044]

JonBenet was a good kid, a happy kid per ▮▮▮▮▮ [5-1350]

6/03/98

JONBENÉT RAMSEY MURDER BOOK SUMMARY INDEX

JonBenet Ramsey

Civilians/Items

▮▮▮▮▮▮▮....Patsy...Why didn't I wake up and hear something.
[5-5370]

▮▮▮▮▮▮▮.... I was still under, there's no possible way these two individuals could have possibly ever, ever, ever, ever have done this. [5-5371]

▮▮▮▮▮▮▮....Patsy was very close to JonBenet...5-5886...One time Patsy said Lets go Lets go ...that was the first time I had actually ever seen her angry at the children at all. [5-5384]

▮▮▮▮▮▮▮....I don't know anybody who personally disliked John Ramsey. [5-5459]

▮▮▮▮▮▮▮....re; the ransom note...I also hold a social work background in adolescent development and a note just strkes me as something an 18-25 year old male would write. [5-5495]

▮▮▮▮▮▮▮....(Kindergarten teacher)....JonBenet is the type of student anybody would love to have in her-in a class. She was - her academics were good and she interacted well with the other children, she was a caring a loving little girl willing to help, just a real nic little girl. (5518)...Patsy seemed to be very close to JonBenet...she seemed to be rather protective of her. [5-5515]

▮▮▮▮▮▮▮....John was 100% dedication to Patsy...John is just perfect...a very kin of a southern person...He's crazy about Patsy...everyon that I know at Access, loves John...He's a very loyal kind of a person...he never had any behavior that is eccentric in nature...they respected him as a leader...I've never known anyone to stable like that...Welll if anything, patsy probably controls him. [5-5545]

Letter from inmate ▮▮▮▮▮▮▮, Federal Penitentiary in Atlanta, GA: "Detective, you do not have a family member or a terrorist killer here. You have a very specialized pedophile. He is sadistic and he is a killer who only preys on young girls. It's obvious to me. I've been there but hidden to others." [8-141]

▮▮▮▮▮▮▮ stated that he's a theif, but not a killer. [26-110]

▮▮▮▮▮▮▮▮▮▮▮▮▮▮▮▮▮▮▮▮▮▮▮

JB not the victim of child abuse. [26-182]

▮▮▮▮▮▮▮▮▮▮▮▮▮▮▮▮▮▮

Per Dr. ▮▮▮▮ and Dr. ▮▮▮, chronic sexual abuse would be a difficult diagnosis. [26-192]

Per Dr. ▮▮▮▮ - it would be definitely a consideration that it could have been caused by a stun gun. [26-192]

Per Dr. ▮▮▮▮ - the application of the stun gun would actually be used in the commission of the crime rather thatn an effort to stage or to throw off the police. [26-193]

Meterorologist ▮▮▮▮ "the snow probably would not have stuck to the pavement because of the high daytime temperature because the pavement would tend to hold the heat in. [26-263]

6/03/98

JONBENÉT RAMSEY MURDER BOOK SUMMARY INDEX

JonBenet Ramsey

Civilians/Items

Ms. ▓▓▓▓, a neighbor, stated that the only suspicious thing that she observed was that the inside of the Ramsey residence in the southeast corner room the light was not on. This was suspicious for the light in that room has been on continuously for the last few years. [1-98]

▓▓▓▓▓▓ stated that he and his brother ▓▓▓▓▓▓ had watched movies at their residence during the evening of 12/25/96 and stayed up late and went to bed at approximately 0100 hours on 12/26/96. Their window directly overlooks the front yard of 755 15th Street. They did not notice anything unusual or see anything suspicious. [1-99]

▓▓▓▓▓▓ stated that the parents of John and Burke did not hit, yell, scream, belittle the children while disciplining them. [1-99]

Mr. ▓▓▓▓, a neighbor, stated that Mrs. Ramsey was a doting mother to JonBenet. Described Mr. Ramsey as being mild mannered. [1-99]

Mr. ▓▓▓▓ a neighbor, stated that on 12/26/96, he observed that a basement door leading into the kitchen area was standing wide open. He thought that this was unusual. [1-100]

Neighbors, Mr. & Mrs. ▓▓▓▓, stated that Mr. Ramsey was very nice and relaxed. [1-100]

Patsy was on the living room floor and was out of it. [1-111]

John Ramsey was drinking scotch. He was sobbing. [1-111]

Why did they do this? Why did they do this? (Patsy Ramsey) [1-112]

"I just want to stay asleep." (Patsy Ramsey) [1-112]

She needs to be supported. Was drousy and dazed. [1-112]

▓▓▓▓▓▓▓▓▓▓▓▓▓▓▓▓▓▓▓▓▓▓▓▓

The Ramsey family is an ideal family. [1-132]

John Ramsey stated "if only I had set the alarm, if only the dog had been in the house." [1-132]

Mrs. Ramsey looked extremely distraught and was barely able to speak. [1-134]

Regarding John Ramsey - he had his arms in his lap and his hands clasped together. He kept his head down and he appeared very agitated. His face was flushed and he ran his hands together several times. [1-137]

Regarding Patricia Ramsey - "Will this help find who killed my baby?" "I did not murder my baby." [1-143]

Regarding Patsy Ramsey - "I'm never coming back." [1-163]

▓▓▓▓▓▓▓▓▓▓▓▓▓▓▓▓▓▓▓▓▓▓▓▓

▓▓▓▓ describes Ramsey's as a loving family. [1-168]

6/03/98

JONBENÉT RAMSEY MURDER BOOK SUMMARY INDEX

JonBenet Ramsey

Civilians/Items

████████, a former teacher of JonBenet, was asked how JonBenet might react to an intruder. She said that she would have kicked, screamed and fought if it was a stranger. She also stated that there was a very positive relationship between JonBent and Patsy, loving and laughing. Also, when John Ramsey dropped JonBenet off, often he would be smiling, talkative, kissing and hugging. [1-768]

Patricia Ramsey made a comment to ███████████ "They've killed my baby and now they're going to kill my husband." [1-784]

According to ██████████, the Ramsey family has no alcohol issues or mental health issues [1-914]

per ████████████, Patsy was very close to JonBenet. [1-1021]

per ████████████ - John Ramsey was surprisingly shy. [1-1024]

███████████ descrives John Ramsey as being quiet, reserved, kind, gentle, intelligent and loyal. Patsy has high energy and involved in activities. Never abuse in the Ramsey home. Does not think John or Patricia Ramsey are involved in teh death of JonBenet. [1-1033]

███████████ thought it strange that Patsy did not move initially when hearing that the body had been found. [1-1194]

John Ramsey would not have worn Hitec foot ware. John always wore penny loafers and nothing else. [1-1249]

███████████ heard a reporter saying that a man with blond hair and glasses was seen at the door of the Ramsey home on 12/25/96. [1-1367]

Det. Harmer's report in talking with Patsy.....John and I did not do this. I don's mind being investigated to a point. [1-1516]

███████████.......JonBenet was a most unusual, gifted student who was very humble and compassionate. Also other children loved JonBenet as she was a very sweet girl. [1-1589]

███████████.....I can't see any of the family being involved. [1-1649]

Per ████████████..... Patsy looked dead herself...was up every 30 minutes thoughout the night. Jon was pacing when I got there...was pacing and crying thoughout the night...Patsy would ask █████ to check on Burke every 10 minutes.. [1-1881]

███████████ said ...you can't hear anything from upstairs. [1-1882]

Per Melinda - "Or I thought it was some weirdo off the street." [5-219]

We've always prayed at dinner times. (Per Melinda) [5-227]

I found a little small kernel size piece of glass and I put it up on the sill. [5-242]

John Ramsey statement upon finding the body - "Oh my god, oh my god." [5-243]

JONBENÉT RAMSEY MURDER BOOK SUMMARY INDEX

JonBenet Ramsey

Civilians/Items

The electrical impulses from stun guns can cause repetitive muscular contractions, numbness, confusion and loss of balance. Voluntary muscle control is interrupted temporarily, leaving the victim dazed, limp and incapacitated for up to 15 minutes. [27-58]

(Interiew). It was clear that Burke was not a witness to JonBenet's death. He woes not appear fearful at home. [32-135]

[1-28(*), 1-29(*), 1-30(*), 1-33(*), 1-48]

6/03/98

CHAPTER 9:

EVIDENCE—BURKE, FRUIT COCKTAIL, INTERVIEW HYSTERIA, FEDERAL JUDGE RULING

The following evidence, although briefly described here, is significant and of vital importance to the case.

BURKE RAMSEY—
INNOCENCE ESTABLISHED EARLY IN THE INVESTIGATION

Burke Ramsey was evaluated by the Boulder Department of Social Services within two weeks of JonBenét's murder. This was a mandatory, state-ruled evaluation dictated by the murder of his sister. Those interviewing Burke were experts in evaluating children in trauma. If they found reason for concern for Burke, he would be removed from his parents. Social Services found no reason to remove him. Burke continued to live with his parents. I obtained a copy of this confidential report. The department findings included a definitive opinion that Burke was not involved in his sister's death. Their conclusion: "From the interview, it is clear Burke was not a witness to JonBenét's death. He does not appear fearful at home."

PINEAPPLE SPECULATION—
POLICE REPORT SUMMARIES.

One of the aspects still most speculated about pertains to a crime scene photo of a bowl of pineapple on a kitchen table. The bowl and spoon had Patsy's and Burke's fingerprints on them. Combining that image with a reference in the autopsy that JonBenét's stomach contained "fragmented pieces of yellow to light green-tan vegetable or fruit material which may represent fragments of pineapple," resulted in massive conjecture with certain Ramsey case police investigators, stirring up entertainment talk shows with theories that this added to Patsy's and John's guilt, and perhaps Burke's guilt. Actual lab testing would follow the autopsy.

Published here for the first time are the actual summary pages of police reports from the JonBenét Murder Book Summary Index. It

This crime scene photograph caused speculation that is still on-going. Police leaks indicated Patsy or Burke killed JonBenét after she allegedly took pineapple from this bowl while Burke was eating from it. Patsy and Burke's fingerprints were on the bowl or the utensil. The information was false based on the actual police reports and lab tests conducted a year after JonBenét was murdered.

includes the testing on JonBenét's stomach and intestine. Of interest: That her stomach and intestine content wasn't taken in for testing until ten months after her murder. The results are listed as being vocalized to a Boulder police investigator one year later, on Christmas Day, 1997. Experts from the University of Colorado, consulted by Boulder police, conducted the tests. The results shown in the index summary clearly indicate that JonBenét's stomach contents include pineapple, grapes, grape skins, and cherries. A forensic coroner told me, "That's what is in a fruit cocktail." There is nothing in the police report summaries I have that indicates whether Boulder police categorized and then listed the food items in the Ramsey kitchen. So the question becomes: Where and when did JonBenét eat fruit cocktail?

I have redacted information about private individuals in this portion of the JonBenét Ramsey Murder Book Summary Index. This is the first time these two pages have been made public. There is no explanation for the long delay in getting the material tested.

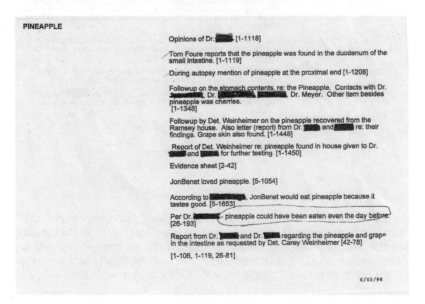

PINEAPPLE

Opinions of Dr. ▓▓. [1-1118]

Tom Foure reports that the pineapple was found in the duodenum of the small intestine. [1-1119]

During autopsy mention of pineapple at the proximal end [1-1208]

Followup on the stomach contents, re: the Pineapple. Contacts with Dr. ▓▓▓▓▓, Dr. ▓▓▓▓▓ ▓▓▓▓▓, Dr. Meyer. Other item besides pineapple was cherries. [1-1348]

Followup by Det. Weinheimer on the pineapple recovered from the Ramsey house. Also letter (report) from Dr. ▓▓ and ▓▓ re: their findings. Grape skin also found. [1-1448]

Report of Det. Weinheimer re: pineapple found in house given to Dr. ▓▓ and ▓▓ for further testing. [1-1450]

Evidence sheet [2-42]

JonBenet loved pineapple. [5-1054]

According to ▓▓▓▓▓, JonBenet would eat pineapple because it tastes good. [5-1653]

Per Dr. ▓▓▓▓ - pineapple could have been eaten even the day before. [26-193]

Report from Dr. ▓▓ and Dr. ▓▓ regarding the pineapple and grape in the intestine as requested by Det. Carey Weinheimer [42-78]

[1-106, 1-119, 26-81]

6/03/98

JonBenet Ramsey

Civilians/Items

December 25, 1996	▓▓▓▓▓▓ said that JonBenet Ramsey didn't have anything to eat at his house because she had crab at her house. [5-3529]
December 30, 1996 10:17	The following items were received into property: pineapple-70KKY; bowl found on north dining room table-71KKY; roll of film-72KKY. [2-42]
October 15, 1997	Det. Sgt. Tom Wickman and Det. Weinheimer met with Dr. ▓▓▓▓ at the University of Colorado about the contents found inside the small intestine. [1-1156]
October 15, 1997	Det. Sgt. Tom Wickman and Det. Weinheimer met with Dr. ▓▓▓▓ at the University of Colorado about the contents found inside the small intestine. [1-1156]
October 15, 1997	Sgt. Wickman and Det. Weinheimer met Dr. ▓▓▓▓ at the University of Colorado and Dr. ▓▓▓▓ concerning the identification of the contents found in JonBenet Ramsey's small intestine. [1-1348]
October 16, 1997 14:45	Det. Weinheimer retrieved the test tube containing the intestine contents from the Coroner's Office. [1-1348]
October 16, 1997 14:59	Det. Weinheimer put the intestine contents into the freezer in the evidence section of the Boulder Police Dept. [1-1348]
October 17, 1997 09:54	Det. Weinheimer checked the intestine contents out of the Boulder Police Dept. evidence and took to to Dr. ▓▓▓▓ office at the University of Colorado. [1-1348]
October 17, 1997 12:01	Det. Weinheimer returned the test tube of intestine contents to the Boulder Police Department evidence lab after observing Dr. ▓▓▓▓ remove approximately 2 grams of substance from the test tube. [1-1349]
November 5, 1997	Det. Weinheimer also discussed with Dr. ▓▓▓ the cronology of events leading up to JonBenet Ramsey's murder as well as the meaning of the pineapple that was located the small intestine and how long it may have been there. [1-1159]
November 5, 1997	Det. Weinheimer also discussed with Dr. ▓▓▓ the cronology of events leading up to JonBenet Ramsey's murder as well as the meaning of the pineapple that was located the small intestine and how long it may have been there. [1-1159]
November 18, 1997	Det. Harmer interviewed Officer Lisa Cooper about the contents in a tupperware container within JonBenet Ramsey's bedroom which Cooper states consisted of popcorn. [1-1104]
December 25, 1997	Dr. ▓▓▓▓ informed Det. Weinheimer that the intestine contents included pineapple and grapes including skin and pulp. [1-1349]
January 22, 1998	Det. Weinheimer received a report from Dr. ▓▓▓ and ▓▓▓ concerning their findings from the examination of the contents of the intestine. [1-1349]

These are the reports on the pineapple found in JonBenét's stomach/intestine area, which testing also included grapes, grape skins, and cherries. Of note: The contents were not taken for testing for more than ten months after the murder.The results of the testing were vocalized on December 25, 1997. A written report was delivered to Boulder police on January 22, 1998, more than one year after her murder.

INTERVIEWS: WHEN WERE THEY INTERVIEWED, WHAT MISSED OPPORTUNITIES WERE THERE FOR INTERVIEWS, WHAT MISBEHAVIOR WAS THERE ABOUT INTERVIEWS?

One continuing piece of incorrect information used against the Ramseys is repeated comments from law enforcement that the Ramseys hadn't given interviews. This was reinforced in that Monday news conference. The information wasn't true. The Ramseys had given interviews to Boulder police in the first days of the investigation, but Boulder police publicly insisted they hadn't.

Boulder News Conference—Monday, December 30, 1996.

"Police, however, have not interviewed JonBenét's parents, John and Patricia Ramsey. 'They're still grief-stricken. They're not in any condition to be interviewed,' Police Department Spokeswoman Leslie Aaholm said."
—*Rocky Mountain News*

"They have been in no condition to be interviewed up to this point, she (Boulder Police Department Spokeswoman Leslie Aaholm) said."—*Boulder Daily Camera*

Here is a list of when the Ramseys were interviewed:

1. First interviews—John Ramsey and Patsy Ramsey—Thursday morning, December 26, 1996. Patsy and John Ramsey were interviewed by Detective Linda Arndt, Detective Fred Patterson, Officer Rick French, Officer Bob Whitson, and other officers. None of the interviews was recorded but were referred

to in police reports. The two detectives had one tape recorder between them, and it was hooked up to the telephone in case a kidnapper called. The interviews were not considered by police as ideal interviews, so they were described as conversations.

2. First interview—Burke Ramsey—Thursday, December 26, 1996. Burke was interviewed by Detective Fred Patterson at the home of a friend where he had been taken that morning to protect him from the chaos in the Ramsey home. He was interviewed without his parents' knowledge.

3. Second interview—John Ramsey—Friday afternoon, December 27, 1996. Detective Linda Arndt and Sergeant Larry Mason interviewed John Ramsey that Friday afternoon. John Ramsey asked for Sergeant Larry Mason to come to the home where he was staying for an interview. Patsy Ramsey was sedated and her physician said she couldn't be interviewed.

4. Third interview—Saturday evening, December 28, 1996. Detective Linda Arndt conducted short interviews with and took handwriting samples from John, Patsy, and Burke at the home where they were staying with friends.

5. First Interview—Saturday evening—Melinda and John Andrew Ramsey were interviewed by police detectives.

Missed opportunities on interviews: Boulder police were with Patsy and John Ramsey constantly from the time JonBenét was reported missing on Thursday morning until Sunday afternoon when the family left for Atlanta for a memorial service. They should have been interviewed during those times.

1. Thursday morning—Patsy and Burke should have been taken to the police station for an examination of their clothing and their bodies and for more extensive interviews by police to eliminate or include them as suspects in the then-missing child case. That wasn't done. John should have been interviewed extensively and his clothing and body examined while he was still at his home.

2. Thursday afternoon—John and Patsy should have been taken to the police station the moment JonBenét's body was found for extensive interrogations. This was a huge blunder by police. The family didn't have attorneys then. John said they had been told to leave the home, which was now a crime scene, but they weren't sure what to do and were trying to find a place to stay. He said, "We would have done whatever they told us to do."

3. Thursday afternoon and overnight—Boulder police were with the Ramseys and were writing reports observing the family behavior. They spoke with friends of the family.

4. Friday morning—This was another opportunity to interview both parents, but no one asked them. Boulder police were still with them after writing reports from their observation of them overnight. The rest of the day and overnight were missed opportunities for interviews.

5. Saturday afternoon before and during DNA testing—Boulder police officers were in the home where the family was staying and could have interviewed them. For DNA testing, the family members were at the sheriff's department. They could have been interviewed then as well, although by then,

one attorney had been hired and may have prohibited any more interviews.

6. Saturday and Sunday—Police remained with the Ramseys constantly that Saturday and Sunday but did not interview them. They did observe them and wrote reports on their activities. They may have been prohibited from interviewing by the one attorney who had been hired for the family at that time.

Misbehavior by police about interviews:

1. Friday, December 27, 1996—The commander of the investigation, John Eller, demanded that the Ramseys report to the Boulder Police Station that day. He told them if they didn't, he would withhold their daughter's body from them until they did.

Homicide expert perspective: "Threatening someone by saying, 'We're not going to give your daughter's body back to you unless you do an interview,' that's just nuts. That's coercive behavior and it's illegal. You can't do that."

2. January, February, March/April, 1997—Boulder police constantly negotiated with the Ramsey attorneys for a formal interrogation (a synonym for interrogation is grilling). An interrogation date was set for January 18, 1997. But Patsy Ramsey became ill and couldn't do that interview. John agreed to go ahead, but police declined to do the interrogation. Additional interrogations were scheduled for April 23 for both Patsy and John. The day before, by email, Boulder authorities unilaterally canceled it. No reason was given. In spite of that cancellation,

they continued to complain about the Ramseys not doing interrogations. After much angst, a new, negotiated date was set for April 30, 1997. Patsy and John agreed to interrogations beginning then.

3. The couple was interrogated again separately on a Tuesday, Wednesday, and Thursday on June 23, 24, 25. The interrogations were initiated by John Ramsey after he wrote to District Attorney Alex Hunter asking for more time to talk with law enforcement after the April 30 interrogations. The Ramsey attorneys' main condition for the June interrogations for both Patsy and John was that Boulder police officers not conduct the interrogations based on their "lack of objectivity and judgment" and their campaign of "leaks and smears" against the Ramseys. The interrogations were videotaped.

"I can't force anyone to talk. It doesn't matter where an interview is. Just get it wherever it is. What matters is that you get the interview and always remember you can't force someone to talk if they don't want to." (Homicide expert perspective.)

Information continued to be leaked or verbalized about the Ramseys failing to give interviews.

FEDERAL JUDGE RULING ON THE CASE

In the twenty-five years since JonBenét was murdered, her parents filed nine slander and libel lawsuits against various media organizations and individuals in the case. John filed a recent and tenth lawsuit against CBS for naming Burke as the killer of his sister. Burke also sued. That case was filed for $900 million in 2016 and settled out of court in 2019.

Two defamation lawsuits were filed against John and Patsy Ramsey by people who thought they were unfairly named as suspects in the couple's book, *The Death of Innocence,* which was published in 2000.

One of those cases, *Wolf vs. Ramsey*, was dismissed before trial by a federal judge and that's the case looked at here. The judge dismissed the case in March of 2003.

Judge Julie E. Carnes from the United States District Court in the Northern District Court of Georgia wrote a highly unusual recital of flaws in the case by those testifying for Robert Christian Wolf, who was suing the Ramseys. She concluded, "The weight of the evidence is more consistent with a theory that an intruder murdered JonBenét than it is with a theory that Mrs. Ramsey did so."

Her dismissal ruling was ninety-three-pages long. It's unusual because of its length from a federal judge, its conclusion, and its detailed analysis of what she outlined as errors in the case against John and Patsy Ramsey. In particular, Judge Carnes debunked the "speculation" by ex-Detective Steve Thomas, who testified for Robert Wolf, and, as described by Judge Carnes in her ruling: "In Mr. Thomas's scenario, rather than being grateful that her child was alive, Mrs. Ramsey nevertheless decided to finish the job off by fashioning a garrote from one of her paintbrushes, looping the cord around the child's neck, and then choking JonBenét to death." More than six years after her murder, with the autopsy and further evidence from JonBenét's bed sheets contradicting bedwetting "speculation," Thomas still testified that Patsy killed JonBenét. Thomas was also criticized by the judge for his views on digestion rates of pineapple in JonBenét's stomach. "Relying solely on the testimony of Mr. Thomas, who has no apparent expertise as a medical examiner, plaintiff fixed the time of death at around one a.m."

In a factual reciting of the evidence in her dismissal ruling, Judge Carnes dismisses the popular allegations of bedwetting as a motive for JonBenét's death noting there was urine in JonBenét's clothes, but "crime scene photos do not indicate JonBenét's sheets were wet or suggest that the sheets to the bed had been changed." Judge Carnes had overseen no other cases on the Ramseys before this one was assigned to her courtroom.

In the Ruling to Dismiss the defamation suit, Judge Carnes also criticized the Boulder Police Department. She censured Wolf's attorney. She dissected the evidence, ultimately concluding that the Ramseys did not kill their daughter.

Judge Carnes was promoted to Chief Federal Judge of the U.S. District for the Northern District of Georgia on January 1, 2009.

Her case analysis would provide a blueprint of blunders for a defense attorney if anyone, including John and Patsy, were ever charged and taken to trial.

Boulder District Attorney Mary Keenan Lacy, who served from January 2001 to January 2009, publicly concurred with the conclusion of Federal District Court Judge Julie Carnes that an "intruder" was a more likely killer than Patsy Ramsey.

CHAPTER 10:

EVIDENCE—
RAMSEY GRAND JURY

The Ramsey grand jury began hearing testimony in September of 1998. It gave its decision to prosecutors on the case in a confidential meeting in October of 1999.

It's critically important to understand the difference between a grand jury and a trial.

A grand jury is a try-out of sorts for a criminal trial. It's a chance for prosecutors to see the evidence, to hear the testimony, and to determine if there is enough to go to trial. The grand jurors hear only what the prosecution wants them to hear, but they have the right to request additional evidence.

A grand jury is designed to be completely one-sided. The prosecutors determine who testifies and who doesn't and what slant the questioning of witnesses will take. There is no defense. None of those who testify are allowed to have their own attorneys question them for clarification. The goal is to test whatever evidence the prosecution presents and to require reluctant witnesses to testify. A grand jury has the power to recommend charges for a criminal trial. The prosecutors then decide if they'll take a case to trial. There is a presumption of fairness, but that doesn't always happen. As was the case with the Ramsey grand jury.

Even though the grand jury proceedings are confidential, what became publicly apparent was that the dysfunction in the Ramsey case continued outside the grand jury courtroom with politics, head-scratching decisions, and questions about agendas. It became a saga about who would testify and who wouldn't. Here's some of that outside maneuvering.

Patsy and John Ramsey. They would be the stars of any grand jury testimony. The must-haves. For nearly two years before the start of the grand jury, within minutes after their daughter's body was found, John and Patsy Ramsey were the suspects in the murder of their daughter. So they, one would think, were key for testimony to this grand jury. They'd even spent several days in interrogations with prosecutors in April of 1997 and June of 1997.

However, neither John Ramsey nor Patsy Ramsey was subpoenaed by prosecutors to testify before the grand jury even though their attorneys said they would testify if subpoenaed. Why wouldn't they be subpoenaed to testify, be questioned without their attorneys to protect them? Why wouldn't prosecutors want to get the answers to all those unknown questions from Patsy and John while they were testifying under oath for however long prosecutors wanted to question them?

The conclusion: The grand jury prosecutors didn't want the grand jurors to hear from the Ramseys.

Yet it wasn't just Patsy and John who weren't welcome before the grand jury.

Add Lou Smit to the list.

Homicide Detective Lou Smit was renowned in his field. He was hired by the Boulder DA in March of 1997 and testified many times before grand juries during his career. He came into the case believing the Ramseys were guilty based on publicity in the case. But once he began studying, organizing, and cataloguing the evidence, Smit did a quick turn-around. He became a believer in the Ramseys' innocence and was vocal about it.

Smit expected to testify before the grand jury because of his extensive homicide experience (over 200 cases) and his alternate opinion on who killed JonBenét. He was shocked, and didn't understand why, he says, when he was told by the chief prosecuting attorney supervising the grand jury that he would not be allowed to testify. Smit's response was to send a letter to the grand jury foreperson asking to appear and testify to present his fact-based opinion that an intruder killed JonBenét.

Within a month, the chief prosecutor supervising the grand jury and District Attorney Alex Hunter wrote Smit a letter saying he couldn't tell anyone about his letter to the grand jurors. They then went to court to bar Smit from testifying at all. Smit fought them in court with his own money and succeeded in testifying before the grand jury. He said he had "never been treated more terribly" by prosecutors when he did testify. He was on the stand for approximately three hours, rather than the eight hours he had asked for to present his opinion.

Why go to extremes to prevent Smit from testifying and ignore Patsy and John Ramsey?

Was this grand jury a rubber stamp that prosecutors were using to present only the "Ramseys Did It" evidence?

That premise is underscored from someone who did testify: One of the people who appeared before the grand jury, Susan Stine, a close friend of the Ramseys, thought the questions she was asked by prosecutors were unfair. "It was very clear to me the prosecutors were out to get the Ramseys. Their questions were filled with alleged facts and evidence that the police and prosecutors should have already known wasn't accurate."

Colorado Springs, CO 80904
January 21, 1999

Grand Jury Foreperson

RE: JonBenet Ramsey Case

Dear Mr. Plese

My name is Lou Smit, a retired detective previously assigned to the JonBenet Ramsey case who resigned from the case in September 1998. I was hired by Alex Hunter in March 1997 to assist his office in organizing and analyzing the case materials presented to his office by the Boulder Police Department. During the 19 months spent in Boulder, I worked very closely with D.A.s Trip DeMuth and Peter Hofstrom. Together we examined all aspects of this case.

I have been in law enforcement for 32 years, have been involved in over 200 homicide investigations and have worked many high-profile cases in Colorado. I was hired because of my experience and background. I take my work very seriously and truly desire to seek justice not only for JonBenet but her parents as well.

I resigned because I do not agree with others in authority, that John and Patsy Ramsey killed their daughter. I see evidence in the case of an intruder, and I cannot in good conscience assist in the prosecution of people I believe to be innocent.

That is why I am writing you this letter. I would respectfully request that I be called to give testimony before the Grand Jury to provide an "intruder" side of the story. Please take the time to consider what I have to say while evaluating the evidence and making such difficult decisions regarding an indictment in this case.

I have prepared a presentation which would take about eight hours of the Grand Jury's time.

Respectfully submitted,

Lou Smit
Retired Detective
719-633-5178

Homicide Detective Lou Smit's letter to the Ramsey Grand Jury foreperson asking to testify. January, 1999.

Three of the most key people in the Ramsey case, people who could add depth and knowledge were not asked to testify. And, as just noted, there was a serious fight to prohibit Lou Smit from testifying.

Just how much control and influence did District Attorney Hunter have over the grand jury hearing the Ramsey case? Not much. Here's why:

The Ramsey case and its breakdown affected people throughout the world. Colorado's governor wasn't immune to the dysfunction. Colorado Governor Roy Romer had been in office for nine years when Jon-Benét Ramsey was murdered. He watched the debacle from his office in Denver. Consequently, he hand-selected four experienced Colorado district attorneys to make recommendations about how to fix the mess with both the police department and the district attorney. Legally, he couldn't replace the Boulder Police Department unless they asked for his help. They refused to do so. But he could make changes in the Boulder District Attorney's Office.

In August of 1998, Hunter walked into a meeting with selected district attorneys for what he thought was a helpful and friendly session where he'd get "a little advice." Instead, he found out that he had to remove the attorneys in his office from the case, or he would be fired. Without much thought, he chose to fire his own attorneys. He also agreed to accept three outside replacement attorneys to run the grand jury. He learned that not only would he not run the grand jury, he would only be allowed to stay on as long as he followed the new grand jury attorney recommendations and accepted low-key decision-making in his new figurehead role. Hunter would still represent his office by fronting the public announcements. The grand jury began hearing the Ramsey case less than a month later, in September of 1998.

In October of 1999, the grand jury recommended two charges against John Ramsey and two charges against Patsy Ramsey. The charges were not disclosed publicly.

The charges were the same:

Accessory to a Crime—Two Counts

Child Abuse Resulting in Death—Two Counts

Neither Patsy nor John was charged with murder. There was considerable speculation that the prosecutors presented a theory that nine-year-old Burke Ramsey killed his sister and his parents covered it up. Yet, there was overwhelming evidence that Burke had not killed his sister, including the social services report saying he was not a "witness to JonBenét's death."

In spite of the grand jury recommendations, and after listening to testimony and looking at crime scenes for just over a year, the three prosecuting attorneys didn't think they would be successful in convicting John and Patsy Ramsey of those charges. They decided to reject the recommended indictments by the grand jurors. They wouldn't go to trial. District Attorney Alex Hunter made the announcement.

The grand jury indictments were released publicly fourteen years later after a judge ordered they be made public. It was October of 2013. At the same time, the judge refused John Ramsey's request to release all the grand jury transcripts to the public so that what evidence was or was not presented to the grand jurors could be fairly judged.

After twenty-eight years in office as the Boulder district attorney, Alex Hunter did not run for office in 2000. He retired.

CHAPTER 11:

EVIDENCE—
DISTRICT ATTORNEY EXONERATION

LACY LETTER TO JOHN RAMSEY

July 9, 2008

Mr. John Ramsey,

As you are aware, since December 2002, the Boulder District Attorney's Office has been the agency responsible for the investigation of the homicide of your daughter, JonBenet. I understand that the fact that we have not been able to identify the person who killed her is a great disappointment that is a continuing hardship for you and your family.

However, significant new evidence has recently been discovered through the application of relatively new methods of DNA analysis. This new scientific evidence convinces us that it is appropriate, given the circumstances of this case, to state that we do not consider your immediate family including you, your wife, Patsy, and your son, Burke, to be under any suspicion in the commission of this crime. I wish we could have done so before Mrs. Ramsey died.

We became aware last summer that some private laboratories were conducting a new methodology described as "touch DNA." One method of sampling for touch DNA is the "scraping method." This is a process in which forensic scientists scrape places where there are no stains or other signs of the possible presence of DNA to recover for analysis any genetic material that might nonetheless be present. We contracted with the Bode Technology Group, a highly reputable laboratory recommended to us by several law enforcement agencies to use the scraping method for touch DNA on the long johns that JonBenet wore and that were probably handled by the perpetrator during the course of this crime.

The Bode Technology laboratory was able to develop a profile from DNA recovered from the two sides of the long johns. The previously identified profile from the crotch of the underwear worn by JonBenet at the time of the murder matched the DNA recovered from the long johns at Bode.

Unexplained DNA on the victim of a crime is powerful evidence. The match of male DNA on two separate items of clothing worn by the victim at the time of the murder makes it clear to us that an unknown male handled these items. Despite substantial efforts over the years to identify the source of this DNA, there is no innocent explanation for its incriminating presence at three sites on these two different items of clothing that JonBenet was wearing at the time of her murder.

Solving this crime remains our goal, and its ultimate resolution will depend on more than just matching DNA. However, given the history of the publicity surrounding this case, I believe it is important and appropriate to provide you with our opinion that your family was not responsible for this crime. Based on the DNA results and our serious consideration of all the other evidence, we are comfortable that the profile now in CODIS is the profile of the perpetrator of this murder.

To the extent that we may have contributed in any way to the public perception that you might have been involved in this crime, I am deeply sorry: No innocent person should have to endure such an extensive trial in the court of public opinion, especially when public officials have not had sufficient evidence to initiate a trial in a court of law. I have the greatest respect for the way you and your family have handled this adversity.

I am aware that there will be those who will choose to continue to differ with our conclusion. But DNA is very often the most reliable forensic evidence we can hope to find and we rely on it often to bring to justice those who have committed crimes. I am very comfortable that our conclusion that this evidence has vindicated your family is based firmly on all of the evidence, including the reliable forensic DNA evidence that has been developed as a result of advances in that scientific field during this investigation.

We intend in the future to treat you as the victims of this crime, with the sympathy due you because of the horrific loss you suffered. Otherwise, we will continue to refrain from publicly discussing the evidence in this case.

We hope that we will one day obtain a DNA match from the CODIS data bank that will lead to further evidence and to the solution of this crime. With recent legislative changes throughout the country, the number of profiles available for comparison in the CODIS data bank is growing steadily. Law enforcement agencies are receiving increasing numbers of cold hits on DNA profiles that have been in the system for many years. We hope that one day soon we will get a match to this perpetrator. We will, of course, contact you immediately. Perhaps only then will we begin to understand the psychopathy or motivation for this brutal and senseless crime.

Respectfully,
Mary T. Lacy
District Attorney
Twentieth Judicial District
Boulder, Colorado

Mary Keenan Lacy was the Boulder district attorney when she wrote this letter to John Ramsey exonerating him, Patsy, and Burke. The letter would be admissible in a trial.

Boulder District Attorney Mary Lacy took office in 2001. She had been with the District Attorney's Office for eighteen years before she was elected district attorney. During her tenure, she was in charge of the sexual assault unit for ten years. As a result, she had extensive experience with DNA in a large number of her cases before she became district attorney, and she continued studying and researching ongoing advances in DNA after her election, believing it was a key to most of her cases as district attorney.

District Attorney Lacy and her office "assumed responsibility" for the Ramsey case in December of 2002. In essence, she took the case away from the Boulder Police Department.

She was known as someone who kept her word. While campaigning to become district attorney, Lacy pledged that if elected she would reduce the number of what were considered troublesome plea bargains in the office and increase the number of trials. And that's what she did. In 2000, before she was elected, there were ten felony trials in Boulder. In 2003, after she took office, there were twenty-four felony trials.[7] The plea bargains versus felony trials were an issue because her predecessor, Alex Hunter, had been publicly criticized by other metro Denver district attorneys for not going to trial, but instead using plea bargains to resolve cases. They felt trials offered more accountability and that wasn't happening in Boulder.

When she was elected district attorney, Lacy told me in an interview, she was concerned about the credibility of law enforcement in Boulder, partially because of the Ramsey case. She wanted more transparency from her office to the public to "enhance credibility." She planned to strengthen the knowledge of some of her colleagues by "increasing the numbers of district attorney employees attending DNA classes like those sourced by the FBI."

Lacy did not comment much about the Ramsey case during her two terms in office. The talking she did came in an impressive July 9, 2008 news release about the results of new "touch DNA" testing in the Ramsey case. She noted "despite a long and intensive investigation, the death of JonBenét remains unsolved. The murder has received unprecedented publicity and has been shrouded in controversy. That publicity has led to many theories over the years in which suspicion has focused on one family member or another. However, there has been at least one persistent stumbling block to the possibility of prosecuting any Ramsey family members for the death of JonBenét— DNA."[8]

As part of the continuing investigation into who killed JonBenét Ramsey, Lacy's office looked at the child's clothing—specifically her long johns—that had not been tested for DNA. With the experience of her sexual assault background guiding them, Lacy and her team decided to submit JonBenét's long johns. They reasoned that her attacker would have had to pull those long johns down before sexually assaulting her. "These sites were chosen because evidence supports the likelihood that the perpetrator removed and/or replaced the long johns, perhaps by handling them on the sides near the waist."[9]

Lacy and her team would have the long johns tested on both sides of the waist, inside and out, using a new "touch DNA" method that they had learned about in their continuing DNA research.

The long johns were submitted for testing in late 2007 at the Bode

Labs located near Washington, D.C. "Touch DNA" was the testing method used.

"On March 24, 2008, Bode informed us that they had recovered and identified genetic material from both sides of the waist area of the long johns. The unknown male profile previously identified from the inside crotch area of the underwear [identified in 1997 from the Colorado Bureau of Investigation testing and additionally in separate testing, from Cellmark Labs], matched the DNA recovered from the long johns at Bode."[10]

Lacy was advised to have additional confirmation testing done after the Bode results and she did so with the Colorado Bureau of Investigation. "We received those results on June 27th of this year [2008] and are, as a result, confident that this DNA did not come from innocent sources at the autopsy."[11]

Lacy believed the new "touch DNA" profile belonged to JonBenét's killer and excluded "any member of the Ramsey family, including John, Patsy or Burke Ramsey, as suspects in this case."[12]

The Ramsey defense attorneys were told about the rumored DNA tests when one of them, Bryan Morgan, was contacted by District Attorney Lacy who told Morgan she had some "remarkable" new DNA test results and she wanted to personally report them to John Ramsey.

Defense attorneys Hal Haddon and Bryan Morgan and their client, John Ramsey, met Lacy in her office. "She invited us to sit down and she addressed John Ramsey face to face directly and candidly. She reported to him what had been done with the DNA testing, what it meant to the investigation, and emphasized it utterly eliminates any Ramseys as suspects in this case," said one of John's attorneys. Lacy went on to say, "We profoundly apologize for the pain this has caused for the

last twelve years to you and your family." The attorney added, "My recollection was that we were all pretty stunned."

"She presented me with the letter exonerating us and apologizing
for the way we had been treated," says John. "There wasn't the relief for
me you would expect. What I was thinking was that now we could focus
on finding the killer and quit trying to prove that it was the Ramseys.
That was so significant and so hopeful."

"We met with the district attorney and her staff at a later point and
it was a brain storming session. We talked about who we could look at,
how we could help, and possibilities other than the family," added John.

The hope of John Ramsey was misplaced. Mary Lacy was jumped
on with a vengeance. The media coverage and talk show opinion were
savage with anger over the exoneration and apology. Lost in the outrage,
was the fact of the DNA finding of a *match* from 2008 "touch DNA"
testing to the 1997 DNA testing by two different agencies.

The columnist David Harsanyi of *The Denver Post*, wrote in July
11, 2008:

**"She [Mary Lacy] has disregarded facts and played the media and
the public for a bunch of suckers along the way. She is trying to do it
again. . . .**

**"But Lacy, one of the most incompetent officials working in Col-
orado law enforcement, has taken us on this ride before. There is
neither the space nor the need to discuss Lacy's ham-fisted ineptitude
here. She is, after all, an elected official, and Boulder voters get what
they deserve."**

Paul Campos of the *Rocky Mountain News* wrote in July 16, 2008:

**"To the many questions that have plagued the Ramsey case
we can now add another: Is Mary Lacy merely incompetent, or is**

something more disturbing going on?"

In 1993, Colorado passed the Victims Rights Act to ensure that crime victims are treated with fairness, respect, dignity and that they are free from intimidation, harassment, and abuse.[12]

Part of Lacy's July 9, 2008 news release declared the Ramsey family as victims and stated: "We believe that justice dictates that the Ramseys be treated only as victims of this very serious crime. We will accord them all the rights guaranteed to the victims of violent crimes under the law in Colorado and all the respect and sympathy due from one human being to another."[13]

What that means in Colorado is that those designated as "victims," as the Ramseys had been by District Attorney Lacy, are also, according to the Colorado Victim's Rights Statute, mandated to get a report once a year on the status of their unsolved crime.

"The law enforcement agency (BPD) on request of the victim shall provide an update at least annually to the victim concerning the status of a cold case." (Colorado Statute 24-4.1-303) The Ramseys have never received a report. Their attorneys have requested one several times.

The next district attorney, Stan Garnett, returned the case to the Boulder Police Department. His predecessor, District Attorney Michael Dougherty has kept the case with Boulder police.

CHAPTER 12:

INSIDER INSIGHTS

While reporting on this case over the last twenty-five years, there is occasional insight that was not published. I'm sharing some of that with you now. It's inside information about nuances in the Ramsey case.

DENVER POLICE CHIEF DAVE MICHAUD
AND HIS OFFER OF HELP TO BOULDER POLICE

Dave Michaud served more than thirty years with Denver Police. He started as a patrol officer. He retired as chief and was the State of Colorado Parole Board chairman when he retired in 2010. He died of cancer on December 31, 2020. He was eighty years old.

He was known as a great chief and excellent cop. As part of my job as an investigative reporter with 9News in Denver, I had known Chief Michaud for several years. One day, after working on the Ramsey case, I stopped by his office to ask him what he knew. It was during the first week. He told me then that he had called and offered help to Boulder Police Chief Tom Koby. "I told him we'll give you one detective or all of our detectives for the Ramsey case and no one needs to know we're involved if that's the way you want it."

He was stunned, he said, when Chief Koby asked him, "What for?"

Denver homicide detectives had experience from hundreds of cases, but Chief Michaud told me Chief Koby refused their offer of help.

Chief Michaud asked me about the comment with this question. "What am I missing?"

PATSY RAMSEY—LAST THOUGHTS

In 2006, months before Patsy Ramsey died from ovarian cancer, she and I would talk briefly about what was most important to her. I agreed to not use her comments until after her death. This is some of what she said:

"I just don't know who killed her. I can't understand that kind of evil. I can't understand why. I can't believe it's someone we know."

"I don't want to die. I don't want to leave. I will be so happy to see JonBenét again. She has such a happy soul. She was a wonderful daughter and friend."

Patsy and John both believe in life after death.

JOHN ANDREW RAMSEY GETS AN APOLOGY

Nearly twenty-five years after JonBenét was murdered, John Andrew was invited to breakfast by Charlie Brennan, a former reporter for the *Rocky Mountain News.* It was early in 2021.

Brennan was the reporter who wrote four exclusive stories early on in the Ramsey case. The four exclusive stories were found to be false. Since they weren't retracted, they became widely publicized as other media organizations reused the inaccurate information in the first months after JonBenét's murder. The four stories were:

1. "John Ramsey is a Pilot and Flew the Family to Georgia in his Plane"

2. "Ransom Demand Equaled the Bonus of the Dead Girl's Dad"

3. "No Footprints in the Snow Caused Police to Suspect the Ramseys"

4. "Handwriting on the Ransom Note Points to Patsy Ramsey"

Brennan admitted to me that he had not asked anyone from the Ramsey team whether his stories were correct. The Ramsey family and their attorneys agree, saying Brennan never contacted them for fact checking. I interviewed Charlie Brennan for my first book about these incorrect stories and he admitted then that he should have trusted his mother who knew the Ramseys and thought they were fine people, as opposed to his police sources, which is what he told John Andrew Ramsey in their breakfast meeting. He also said he relied on one source for one of the stories.

JOHN ANDREW RAMSEY

"I got a breakfast invitation from a reporter who covered the case extensively. I willingly accepted it because I want to talk to all sorts of people. My hope is that knowledgeable people can help out. What I said to this reporter and others is that I feel like we're all veterans of the same war. We all want to see the same thing happen. Find the killer. Get to the bottom of this. Hopefully he can help. He knows the politics. He knows the people. He's been around the block."

That's what John Andrew pitched to the reporter he could have easily despised. But John Andrew's pitch was not why the reporter said he invited John Andrew to meet.

"It was something that he brought up. He had thought about it. Seemed sincere. He simply said 'I want to apologize for things I've written in the past. My mother went to church with your parents. She's been to their home. She told me early on '"Hey, these are good people."'"

The reporter continued, "At the same time, I was listening to people in the police department that I respected and trusted and unfortunately that was the path I took. I should have listened to my mother."

Brennan's stories became a successful and unfortunate part of the deliberate and incorrect leaks agenda begun by Boulder police and the District Attorney's Office to influence the media and public that Patsy and John killed their daughter. The plan began with incorrect information released in the police news conference on December 30, 1996, after JonBenét Ramsey's murder. Brennan's stories were published in early 1997, on January 1, January 22, March 11, and March 19.

DENVER POST SPECIAL EDITION THAT ALMOST WAS

One newspaper reporter and editor told me that in the initial weeks after JonBenét's murder, and based on confidential conversations with Boulder District Attorney Alex Hunter, the *Post* had gone to considerable effort to write up a "Special Edition" on the Ramsey case. A Special Edition is ready to be published anytime during the day, as opposed to the regularly scheduled morning publishing deadline. Remember, this was before online news. The Special Edition was a big deal, ready to go, and just waiting for the headline "John Ramsey is

Arrested." The district attorney told *Post* reporters that the DA's office was only days and maybe hours away from arresting John Ramsey for murdering his daughter. DA Hunter was so convincing to *Post* reporters, the paper wanted to be ready and was. The arrest never happened.

"LEAKS" ABOUT "UNTRUE LEAKS"

The rumors, innuendo, and leaking were so bizarre that finally there were "leaks" about who was behind the "untrue leaks."

Leading candidates included an FBI agent who was accused of orchestrating the leaks. The FBI wasn't involved in the case after JonBenét's body was found.

The other candidate was a psychiatrist who befriended Boulder District Attorney Alex Hunter. He was accused of managing the "incest" campaign against John Ramsey.

JOHN ANDREW RAMSEY, BOULDER, THE TOWN, AND HOW THEY AFFECTED THE FAMILY AND THE CASE.

John Andrew Ramsey said he always felt his family was shadow boxing with those who lived in Boulder and its government.

"The people in Boulder and law enforcement just wanted her murder to go away. You have to look at Boulder and the brand that is Boulder—health, exercise, rock climbing, bike riding, running. We are immune from the normal problems of life was the way they seemed to look at it. Life is great. The Ramsey case should just go away."

"The Ramseys ruined the brand. That's what people in Boulder thought. Therefore, it wasn't a reflection on Boulder that their daughter was killed. The problems were in place before the murder with this family, with the child beauty pageants, and what came with them. It's still not something that happens in Boulder."

CHAPTER 13:

CONTINUING INTEREST

Social media and JonBenét Ramsey's murder took some time to collide but when they did, the opinions around the world quickly and firmly divided into two camps. "The Ramseys Killed JonBenét" or "An Intruder Did It" were common statements in online forums.

Sideline opinions ruled as fascination and popularity exploded in new venues dedicated to JonBenét Ramsey: Who killed her? What happened? Here's what I think happened! All of that mattered to people who genuinely wanted others to know what they thought. And now they had places for their opinions to be read.

JonBenét was killed in December of 1996. The World Wide Web was just getting started. Not everybody had a home computer then. Cell phones were pretty much used just for talking. Websites were rare as were chat forums.

Once online sites got started, how long would a topic like JonBenét's murder last? Twenty-five years after her murder, how many Facebook groups do you think are dedicated to trying to solve the JonBenét Ramsey murder?

How many people are involved in those groups would you estimate?

There are twenty-two Facebook groups that I could find. Additionally, there are two Facebook pages and three forums. Nearly

26,000 people are involved with the Ramsey case on Facebook.

"I'm surprised it isn't double or triple that given the twenty-five-year overall media presence the Ramsey case has had. There's the emergence of podcasts and other social media platforms. There are substantial increases in True Crime, especially cold cases," says Ian Greenwood, a PhD candidate in sociology at Colorado State University, with an emphasis in crime, law, and deviance. He's very familiar with the Ramsey case and social media coverage of it.

Social media sites vary. Of those that allow active participation, a few of those groups are marked "closed" and won't allow new members. Some are dedicated to the "Ramseys Did It" theory. Other groups advocate that "An Intruder Did It." Some declare themselves open to all opinions. Participants are removed from the sites and can be banned if their comments don't meet the standards of the administrators of a particular site. Here's an example of a few recent and divided comments:

"When I feel lost in my thoughts, I think about the Ramseys and their constant faith and it restores my trust in God."

"What woman in her 40s, who's already worn out from intense cancer treatments, goes to bed around midnight after running around all day. For that matter, Patsy was said to never wear the same outfit two days in a row, and she suddenly decides to put on the same clothes she wore yesterday?"

"Money talks. They bought the DA's office off. We know that must have been the case."

"I strongly believe JonBenét's father had sold her to some very wealthy man to be exploited sexually. In the process, she died because she was too young to withstand that."

Twenty-five years later, the entertainment and mystery of who killed her continues to intrigue. There are steady numbers of people involved in active participation on social networking and social media sites.

Reddit claims 40,000 members on its closed site.

Twitter has various sites to join in the discussion.

Instagram lists six sites with more than 16,000 active participants.

On YouTube, you can find videos created about JonBenét and documentaries from throughout the years.

"I think part of the fascination with the Ramsey case is the problem with the way the case was reported, how it was reported in the media, the contradictions that were originally laid out in the case," Greenwood says. "It created space for the kind of thought that 'Hey, I have an opinion on what the answer is.' And that's what caused the increase in these social media forums.

"People are actively participating and becoming engaged in the case. They are attached to this mystery, and to solving this case. Most of us are naturally curious and as you lay out a bunch of information, people can have an open public conversation about it and then generate new ideas that otherwise wouldn't be heard."

Comparing online formats with books shows a big difference in interest. More than thirty books published about JonBenét are listed online. Most were published in 2016, which is the twenty-year anniversary of her death. They didn't necessarily sell well. One book sold only seven hardcover copies. Several recorded hardcover sales of fewer than one hundred. E-book sales weren't listed or available.

In 2021, two documentaries so far have aired on the JonBenét murder. One is a news documentary that has been streaming on Discovery+ since January 4, 2021, called *JonBenét Ramsey: What Really Happened*. The other documentary aired on *20/20* on January 15, 2021. It's titled: *JonBenét Ramsey: The List*. Both are two hours long.

As of June 2021, those are the only two documentaries that have aired about JonBenét Ramsey and the twenty-fifth anniversary of her murder. The date for the twenty-fifth anniversary of her murder is December 26, 2021.

CHAPTER 14:

JONBENÉT—WHO SHE WAS

JonBenét wrote this out for her mom and dad eleven months before she was murdered. "I love u love JonBenét" "Thank you for taking me to church."

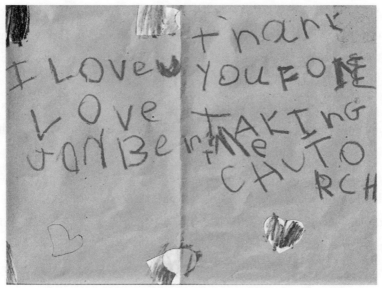

Gone.

It's a brutal and unforgiving word. Accepting its meaning will shatter your life. "Gone" forces the realization that things will never be the same again. The integral person who helped shape your existence will never be there to talk with you, to make you laugh, to just be with you. And imagine how unbearable it would be if part of "gone" includes knowing the person you loved suffered as she died.

JonBenét always made an impression. She was the one who stood out in the room, partly for her appearance, but mostly for what was on the inside of this little girl. She had been given the gift of beauty. She also was given the gifts of self-assurance, joy, and intelligence. The world was a wonderful place for JonBenét and those in it with her. Then, suddenly, with no warning, it wasn't.

Her half-brother, John Andrew Ramsey, realizes he's looking back twenty-five years. The memories, though, are strong and include Jon-Benét playing outside with her brother and defying expectations of a child beauty pageant queen.

"She was an energetic and very outgoing kid. I remember her as a bit of a tomboy and hanging out with Burke and his friends and the boys in the neighborhood.

"What a fun child . . . the spark in the family. She really enjoyed the pageant events and loved being up on stage. She enjoyed being a kindergartner and her artwork in those classes. Really, in remembering her, she enjoyed everything she did.

"What is being portrayed in the public is almost a caricature and that's not her at all. I don't think people understand that mostly she was just a six-year-old who was in kindergarten. She had hobbies. She was not primarily a beauty queen. She was not primarily a pageant queen. But acceptance of her as only that allows one to disassociate from this little girl who was taken from her bed on Christmas and violently assaulted and murdered."

Looking at her report cards shows a kindergartner who got way more plusses than minuses. She was someone her teachers counted on to help out. One of them asked her to walk another child to the school nurse. "She had experience with people being sick with her mother so sick from cancer. So she was kind and understanding." Those words, kind and understanding, about JonBenét were expressed by more than one teacher.

She liked to have fun. JonBenét and a teacher happened to see each other in the hallway and they walked toward each other and joined up. JonBenét's feet were on top of the teacher's feet, the teacher was going forward, JonBenét walking backward, and both were "laughing all the way."

The teachers I talked with didn't know she was in beauty pageants. It wasn't how they identified her.

"I wonder why it's so hard for people to understand this about her," says her father, John. "What an amazing child she was. Sure, she's my daughter and I'm going to feel that way, but it's more than that. For her, beauty pageants were a way for her to play dress up and to perform. That's what it meant to her. What little girl doesn't love that?" Her dad is reminded of what Patsy said about JonBenét and that JonBenét considered pageants normal, fun, and part of play time. "That's just the way it was."

John's wife, Jan, never knew JonBenét. She and John were married in 2014, eight years after Patsy died of ovarian cancer.

"From what I hear, that child was absolutely full of life and fun and joy. I'm struck by all of the photos of JonBenét with a friend and she always had her arm around the shoulder of that other child. She took a position of leadership in friendships and I think she would have been a very, very likeable woman with lots of friends."

Jan says John is unable to think about JonBenét beyond who she was, but not who she might become. "He never talks about what her age would be now or how old she would be. She's frozen in his mind as six years old and the little girl. I think he just misses that little girl and those memories together."

Those memories, John Andrew knows, are so hard for a father remembering his daughter. "That was his youngest child and his daughter and as a father of a daughter, I can tell you about the special relationship you have with your daughter. They think you do no wrong and I think that's been especially hard for him just remembering that adoring little girl."

Jan takes special care of where they are and who they're around. There are times, when she sees a blond child with a ponytail, similar in age to JonBenét, and she reroutes John so he doesn't see her. Here's the reason:

"We were sitting at a restaurant once and a cute little girl jumped from family member to family members' laps. Her blond ponytail was bouncing and she was excited and laughing. I didn't realize John was still so sensitive. That was right after we were married. After the family left the restaurant, John just burst out sobbing. He took two very hard prolonged sobs, then he paused and took a deep breath, and he smiled and shook his head and said to me, 'I'm OK. I'm OK.'"

There is a great sense of profound loss with all of them about JonBenét's death.

"A lot of the difficulty just brings back this flood of emotion. I think of losing my sister, Beth, suddenly in a car accident, and the trauma of that," says John Andrew. "You assume when you lose someone young in life, that it won't happen again. There's just this assumption. It's not going to happen again and then for this to happen, it becomes surreal."

So they continue to do what they are doing to help in trying to find JonBenét's killer. They will do the interviews, look at the suspect possibilities, and spend what has become wearying time remembering. Their lives are not to be envied. These are people who invariably and consistently inhabit a place only they can see. It's where they yearn for a suspect, a reason, an ending, for hope. It's not someplace you want to be. It's part of their loyalty and love for this child, this JonBenét. It's part of their belief that just maybe a great wrong can be righted.

John Andrew believes the case has languished for years. "It is past time to remove the case from the Boulder police. This is about finding a sadistic child killer who has never been caught. We can't expect Boulder police and the very same detectives who have been on the case for twenty-five years to do the right thing and honestly and aggressively investigate who might have killed JonBenét. Is it lack of experience, group think, sheer stupidity, or a concerted effort to conceal the truth? I don't know what these guys are thinking, but the investigation continues to be a massive failure." John Andrew is angry that politics have ruled the investigation and still are. "Personal interest and self-preservation continue to be the through-line of this tragedy, including those who could be making a difference in the case."

And that's what his dad believes. But John is dealing with an additional truth. What is always there for him is that he is now and always will be the father of a murdered child. "If I see a little girl holding hands with her dad, it hurts. That could have been and was JonBenét and me. For the most part, you don't get over it. You move on. A mother who lost a child told me, 'I have a hole in my heart that won't heal' and that was a good way to put it. After JonBenét was murdered, my will to live was definitely challenged. It was agony with that loss and pain. You try to make new memories and you do make new memories and those are good to fall back on and remember. But you don't get over it."

JonBenét and Burke.

JonBenét and a friend.

JonBenét and a friend.

JonBenét and a friend.

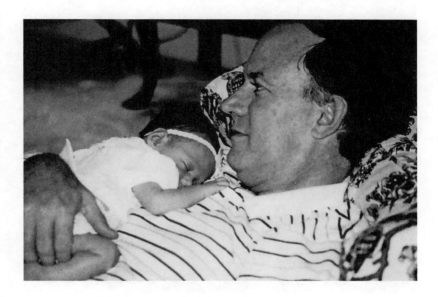

John and baby JonBenét.

JonBenét and Patsy.

JonBenét in Charlevoix, Michigan.

JonBenét and Patsy.

JonBenét, Burke, and Grandmother.

JonBenét in pageant, 1996.

JonBenét in pageant, 1996.

JonBenét in Charlevoix, Michigan.

JonBenét's bible.

Some of JonBenét's stuffed animals.

One of JonBenét's favorite books.

ENDNOTES

1 The Reddit.com interview with Mark Beckner is published in its entirety in my first book on the Ramsey case, *We Have Your Daughter* and on www.paulawoodward.net.

2 Newspaper and television reporting online was rare during this time in 1996 and 1997, so statements were in some cases made one day and reported the next. That's what is reflected.

3 The information comes from an individual count of the articles in Newspapers.com and the Denver Public Library newspaper archives.

4 Information is obtained from the JonBenét Ramsey Murder Book Summary Index, the Boulder Officer Activity Index, and the Boulder First-Responder Police Reports. All were obtained and verified by this author. The evidence listed is from these sources.

5 This information was obtained from a walk-through I did of the Ramsey home, including counting the windows, doors, and locks.

6 The Smit team has a Go-Fund Me account that pays expenses for DNA processing.
https://gofundme.com/f/JonBenét-LouSmit-family-searches-for-justice
The podcast address for the Smit granddaughters is:
https://podcasts.apple.com/dk/podcast/the-victims-shoes/id1500429431

7 Boulder District Attorney's Office, 2004.

8 Boulder District Attorney's Office News Release, July 9, 2008.

9 Ibid.

10 Ibid.

11 Ibid.

12 Colorado Victims Rights Act, 1993, Statute 24-4.

13 Boulder District Attorney's Office News Release, July 9, 2008.

ACKNOWLEDGMENTS

So many people have helped and been there when needed in the writing of this book. Here are a few of them.

Frank Scandale emphasized why I needed to write a book on the twenty-fifth anniversary of JonBenét's terrible murder. His words resonated and convinced me. Thanks, Frank for being such a good listener, friend, and for all the times we worked together at the beginning of this incredible and destructive case.

Chris Lopez was my editor. He and I talked through the verification of documents, the desire by crucial people utilized in my book to remain anonymous and why. We examined the evidence repeatedly, the logic of it, and its value to readers. Chris worked at *The Denver Post* at the beginning of the Ramsey case and throughout the first years, so he had essential knowledge that added value and perspective. Thanks, Chris. You're savvy and logical and were so very helpful and encouraging.

To Jeremy Townsend and MaryAnne Talbot—my copyeditors. Thanks for being smarter than I was when it was most needed.

And to David Wilk—Wow. We're doing it again.

Hayden Clarke was my primary researcher. He was the one who diligently and expertly plowed through the newspaper articles and gave concise and needed perspective.

Wendy Ewaschuk is another researcher who was accurate, honest, and so very gracious. Thanks Wendy. I respect all the information you have collected on the case and your willingness to share.

Cortney Myers was one of those people I called when I was having technical problems and said "help," and she would always say "sure," regardless of how busy she was. You work hard Cortney. You're charming and sharp.

Quincy Newell was my new entertainment attorney on the book. Quincy, you are precise, astute, and understood the deadlines when we were getting my contract resolved. I look forward to doing business with you in the future.

Alan and Lani Dill are two people I treasure. They are two of the most important and remarkable friends I have. Thank you for being there for me with Steve's passing when my need was so great and thank you for continuing with me as such great friends.

Sydney, you understood instantly when I could and couldn't interact because of book deadlines. You always encouraged me and were proud of me when I needed it most. You are smart, creative and always thoughtful. I love and adore you, Syd. (And thanks for going skiing with me.) I learn from you and have great respect for your values. And I love your Winston.

Marc, you are so valuable to so many, especially me, because you are smart, insightful, and wise. You have guided me through some really tough times. You handle so much with dignity and grace. I respect, admire, love, and adore you.

To police officers and law enforcement throughout our country and our world. Thank you for what most of you do on a daily basis with dignity and honor. You are the thin blue line that keeps us safe and separates us from chaos. I believe in you. And to the detectives who helped on my book, you have my complete gratitude for your time, your perspective, your patience, your dedication, your friendship, and for how very smart you are.

My family: the nieces, the greats, all of you. Thank you. Your support and opinions are so important and appreciated. The individual words of wisdom, the confidences, the times you understood this process for me called life, just your being there as a member of my family. You so matter, each and every one of you, and our memories together. We sure have fun.

Holder and Wyatt. Thanks for your help on this book.

And to those life-long friends of mine from high school, college, my career. Love you. Thank you for your friendship and guidance always. I am proud you are my friends.

WEBSITE

www.paulawoodward.net

This website contains information about both books I wrote on the Ramsey case. It includes documents, evidence, photographs and drawings of JonBenét, including the additional information listed below.

Unsolved: The JonBenét Ramsey Murder 25 Years Later, Published October 26, 2021

We Have Your Daughter: The JonBenét Ramsey Murder Twenty Years Later, Published September 27, 2016

On the website:

- New unpublished photos and belongings of JonBenét.
- More written research on just how vast the spread of incorrect information was by certain Boulder police officers.
- An unedited video interview I did with Patsy and John Ramsey early in the case.
- A video tour of the Ramsey home with two detectives including audio. This was within six months of the murder.
- The 911 audio of Patsy Ramsey's desperate call to police on December 26, 1996. I've also included a transcript.
- Federal Judge Julie Carnes 2003 93-page Order dismissing a libel case against Patsy and John Ramsey. The judge lists her reasons for dismissal of the case before trial in the extensive ruling. To me, it's

fascinating and insightful reading. It's considered unusual because of its length, it's by a federal judge, and because of her blunt assessments of some of those testifying.

- The full autopsy of JonBenét Ramsey, which was fully released in August of 1997.
- An unsolicited letter to Patsy Ramsey by a Vassar College professor. He tells her he has no questions that she is "innocent." When she doesn't respond, he offers himself to the Boulder Police Department, which hires him based on his belief and reasoning on why Patsy Ramsey 'did' kill her daughter. His being discovered and the depths he went to so he could be part of the case offer you some perspective on the deception people used to become involved in the case.
- BPD Commander Bob Whitson's police reports.
- We're setting up a system so that I can communicate with my readers on the website.

DOCUMENTS

This is the news release from July 9, 2008, issued by Boulder District Attorney Mary Lacy exonerating the Ramseys based on DNA and apologizing to them.

DISTRICT ATTORNEY S OFFICE
TWENTIETH JUDICIAL DISTRICT

MARY T. LACY, DISTRICT ATTORNEY

July 9, 2008

Boulder District Attorney Mary T. Lacy issued the following announcement with regard to the investigation of the murder of JonBenet Ramsey.

On December 25-26, 1996, JonBenet Ramsey was murdered in the home where she lived with her mother, father and brother. Despite a long and intensive investigation, the death of JonBenet remains unsolved.

The murder has received unprecedented publicity and has been shrouded in controversy. That publicity has led to many theories over the years in which suspicion has focused on one family member or another. However, there has been at least one persistent stumbling block to the possibility of prosecuting any Ramsey family members for the death of JonBenet - DNA.

As part of its investigation of the JonBenet Ramsey homicide, the Boulder Police identified genetic material with apparent evidentiary value. Over time, the police continued to investigate DNA, including taking advantage of advances in the science and methodology. One of the results of their efforts was that they identified genetic material and a DNA profile from drops of JonBenet's blood located in the crotch of the underwear she was wearing at the time her body was discovered. As has previously been reported from various sources, that genetic profile belongs to a male and does not belong to anyone in the Ramsey family.

The police department diligently compared that profile to a very large number of people associated with the victim, with her family, and with the investigation and has not identified the source, innocent or otherwise, of this DNA. The Boulder Police and prosecutors assigned to this investigation in the past also worked conscientiously with laboratory analysts to obtain better results through new approaches and additional tests as they became available. Those efforts ultimately led to sufficient markers from this male profile to enter it into the national DNA data bank.

In December of 2002, the Boulder District Attorney's Office, under Mary T. Lacy, assumed responsibility for the investigation of the JonBenet Ramsey homicide. Since then, this Office has worked with the Boulder Police Department to continue the investigation of this crime.

In early August of 2007, District Attorney Lacy attended a Continuing Education Program in West Virginia sponsored by the National Institute of Justice on Forensic Biology and DNA. The presenters discussed successful outcomes from a new methodology described as "touch DNA." One method for sampling for touch DNA is the "scraping method." In this process, forensic scientists scrape a surface where there is no observable stain or other indication of possible DNA in an effort to recover for analysis any genetic material that might nonetheless be present. This methodology was not well known in this country until recently and is still used infrequently.

In October of 2007, we decided to pursue the possibility of submitting additional items from the JonBenet Ramsey homicide to be examined using this methodology. We checked with a number of Colorado sources regarding which private laboratory to use for this work. Based upon multiple recommendations, including that of the Boulder Police Department, we contacted the Bode Technology Group located near Washington, D.C., and initiated discussions with the professionals at that laboratory. First Assistant District Attorney Peter Maguire and Investigator Andy Horita spent a full day with staff members at the Bode facility in early December of 2007.

The Bode Technology laboratory applied the "touch DNA" scraping sampling technique to both sides of waist area of the long johns that JonBenet Ramsey was wearing over her underwear when her body was discovered. These sites were chosen because evidence supports the likelihood that the perpetrator removed and/or replaced the long johns, perhaps by handling them on the sides near the waist.

On March 24, 2008, Bode informed us that they had recovered and identified genetic material from both sides of the waist area of the long johns. The unknown male profile previously identified from the inside crotch area of the underwear matched the DNA recovered from the long johns at Bode.

We consulted with a different DNA expert, who recommended additional investigation into the remote possibility that the DNA might have come from sources at the autopsy when this clothing was removed. Additional samples were obtained and then analyzed by the Colorado Bureau of Investigation to assist us in this effort. We received those results on June 27th of this year and are, as a result, confidant that this DNA did not come from innocent sources at the autopsy. As mentioned above, extensive DNA testing had previously excluded people connected to the family and to the investigation as possible innocent sources.

I want to acknowledge my appreciation for the efforts of the Boulder Police Department, Bode Laboratory, the Colorado Bureau of Investigation, and the Denver Police Department forensic laboratory for the great work and assistance they have contributed to this investigation.

The unexplained third party DNA on the clothing of the victim is very significant and powerful evidence. It is very unlikely that there would be an innocent explanation for DNA found at three different locations on two separate items of clothing worn by the victim at the time of her murder. This is particularly so here because the matching DNA profiles were found on genetic material from inside the crotch of the victim's underwear and on both sides near the waist of her long johns and because concerted efforts that might identify a source, and perhaps an innocent explanation, were unsuccessful.

It is therefore the position of the Boulder District Attorney's Office that this profile belongs to the perpetrator of the homicide.

3

DNA is very often the most reliable forensic evidence
we can hope to find during a criminal investigation. We
rely on it often to bring to justice those who have
committed crimes. It can likewise be reliable evidence
upon which to remove people from suspicion in appropriate
cases.

The Boulder District Attorney's Office does not
consider any member of the Ramsey family, including John,
Patsy, or Burke Ramsey, as suspects in this case. We make
this announcement now because we have recently obtained
this new scientific evidence that adds significantly to the
exculpatory value of the previous scientific evidence. We
do so with full appreciation for the other evidence in this
case.

Local, national, and even international publicity has
focused on the murder of JonBenet Ramsey. Many members of
the public came to believe that one or more of the Ramseys,
including her mother or her father or even her brother,
were responsible for this brutal homicide. Those
suspicions were not based on evidence that had been tested
in court; rather, they were based on evidence reported by
the media.

It is the responsibility of every prosecutor to seek
justice. That responsibility includes seeking justice for
people whose reputations and lives can be damaged
irreparably by the lingering specter of suspicion. In a
highly publicized case, the detrimental impact of publicity
and suspicion on people's lives can be extreme. The
suspicions about the Ramseys in this case created an
ongoing living hell for the Ramsey family and their
friends, which added to their suffering from the
unexplained and devastating loss of JonBenet.

For reasons including those discussed above, we
believe that justice dictates that the Ramseys be treated
only as victims of this very serious crime. We will accord
them all the rights guaranteed to the victims of violent
crimes under the law in Colorado and all the respect and

4

sympathy due from one human being to another. To the
extent that this office has added to the distress suffered
by the Ramsey family at any time or to any degree, I offer
my deepest apology.

The following Boulder Police Department documents include information only from the morning of December 26, 1996, the day JonBenét's body was found.

The first report is written by the first police responder on the scene: Officer Rick French.

BOULDER POLICE DEPARTMENT
FIELD REPORT
NARRATIVE AND SUPPLEMENT

Page No. 4   CASE NO. P96-21871

DATE OF REPORT (mo./day/year)	TIME	COMPLAINANT-VICTIM
2-26-96	2254	RAMSEY

NARRATIVE

X-STOLEN   D-DAMAGED   R-RECOVERED

DESCRIPTION	SERIAL	UCR	VALUE (LOSS)	RECOVERED

1 friends of the Ramsey's arrived at the house. By 0650 OFC Weiss and OFC Barklow were

2 photographing and fingerprinting areas of the house, and OFC Veitch had collected the

3 ransom note. Reverend ███████ of St. John's Episcopal church in Boulder came

4 to the house at 0713. joining Victim Advocates ███ and ███ in the house with

5 the others. Detectives Linda Arndt and Fred Patterson arrived at the house at about

6 0810 hours.

7   I was concerned with gathering information from Mr. and Ms. Ramsey. They told me

8 that they had spent Christmas night with the ███, and that they arrived home at

9 2200 hours. Mr. Ramsey said he read to both kids for a short time and then they were

10 in bed by 2230 hours. Ms. Ramsey said that Jonbenet had been dressed in white long

11 underwear and a red turtleneck. Jonbenet's and Burke's bedrooms are separate and are

12 located on the second floor of the three story house, with the master bedroom on the

13 top floor. Jonbenet's bedroom has an access door to a second floor porch which was

14 locked and undamaged.

15   As Mr. Ramsey made preliminary telephone calls to gather the demanded amount of

16 money he told me that the only other people with keys to the house are their house-

17 keeper. ███████. and two relatives in Atlanta, Ga. Ms. Ramsey told me that ███

18 ███had spoken to her by telephone on the morning of the 24th and asked for a loan

19 of two thousand dollars. ███ had called again later that day and seemed upset about

20 an arguement with her sister. and she made plans with Ms. Ramsey to come by the Ramsey's

21 house while they were out of town and pick up a check which the Ramsey's would leave for

22 them.

23   When ███████, Patricia Ramsey's mother, was advised by telephone of the

24 incident. she asked that the officers on scene be told of ███████ often

25 commenting on how beautiful Jonbenet was and if Ms. Ramsey was concerned about her

26 being kidnapped. Mrs. Paughs comments were relayed to me by ███████.

12/87 BPD-8

FIELD REPORT
NARRATIVE AND SUPPLEMENT

CASE NO.		P96-21871

Page No. 5

DATE OF REPORT (mo./day/year)	TIME	COMPLAINANT-VICTIM
12-36-96	2317	RAMSEY

NARRATIVE

X-STOLEN   D-DAMAGED   R-RECOVERED

	DESCRIPTION	SERIAL	UCR	VALUE (LOSS)	RECOVERED
1	These factors relating to ▮▮▮ were given to DET Arndt and she began to				
2	develop background information on ▮▮▮. Ms. Ramsey told me further that ▮▮▮				
3	▮▮▮ lived in Ft. Lupton with her husband, ▮▮▮, and a 12 year old daughter.				
4	▮▮▮. Hoffman also has two adult daughters in their twenties, ▮▮ and ▮▮▮, and				
5	she rents the house she lives in from her sister. (Unknown name.)				
6	Two other possible suspects were given by the Ramsey's. One was an ex-employee				
7	who had been fired during the past summer, and had threatened to "bring down Access				
8	Graphics," Mr. Ramsey's business. His name is ▮▮▮. Mr. Ramsey contacted his				
9	personnel department to gather information on ▮▮▮ for the detectives.				
10	The second person mentioned was ▮▮▮ (H: ▮▮▮), who lives in				
11	Louisville. She was Jonbenet's nanny up until two years ago and had a very close				
12	relationship with her. This relationship was the only reason ▮▮▮ was mentioned as				
13	the Ramsey's were trying to allow for all possiblities.				
14	Between times of consulting with the detectives and the family I walked through				
15	the lower level of the house and the garage, looking for obvious evidence. Although				
16	somewhat messy due to the season the residence did not look out of order. In the				
17	basement I attempted to open the door leading to the area where Jonbenet was ultimately				
18	found but it was secured by a wooden latch above the door. The door opened inward and				
19	I was looking for access out of the house. Since the door could not have been used				
20	for that purpose, and it was latched closed, I did not open it.				
21	Shortly after DET SGT Whitson arrived at the house, after 1000, I was released				
22	from the scene and went to the PD to begin the original report.				
23	Just after 1300 hours I heard radio traffic concerning a 911 call and the discovery				
24	of a code black body at the residence, and I returned to 755 15th with OFC Morgan. I				
25	spoke with ▮▮▮, and he told me that Jonbenet had been found in the basement by				
26	Mr. Ramsey while ▮▮, ▮▮▮, and Mr. Ramsey were looking through the house. Mr.				

12/87 BPD-8

Reporting Officer: R. FRINIH   No. 644   Supervisor Approval: 1 65-

FIELD REPORT
NARRATIVE AND SUPPLEMENT

		CASE NO.
	Page No. 6	P96-21571

DATE OF REPORT (mo./day/year)	TIME	COMPLAINANT-VICTIM
12-36-96	2344	Ramsey

NATIVE

X-STOLEN   D-DAMAGED   R-RECOVERED

DESCRIPTION	SERIAL	UCR	VALUE (LOSS)	RECOVERED

1. ▮ told me that he had opened the door to that area earlier in the morning and had
2. not seen Jonbenet's body inside. I secured the area around where Mr. Ramsey had laid
3. the body and assisted in getting the family and friends out of the house to close
4. the crime scene. I left the house for the second time at approximately 0345 hours, and
5. OFCs Weiss and Schunk were securing the front and back, respectively.
6.
7. Burke Ramsey was awakened by his father shortly after ▮ arrived and
8. he was taken to the ▮ residence as soon as he was dressed. I did not speak to
9. him other than to walk him to Mr. ▮ vehicle. He seemed confused and was crying,
10. and Mr. Ramsey again told me that he had slept through the night.

11. EVIDENCE: See PCR's concerning collection by OFCs Veitch, Weiss and Barklow.

13. CONCLUSION: Preliminary indications of the abduction of Jonbenet Ramsey from the
14. residence give way upon the discovery of her body in the residence. A homicide
15. investigation is begun and continued by detectives, with the reclassification of this
16. incident to be forthcoming.

should this be "1545" hrs?

Reporting Officer: Rick French   No. 644   Supervisor Approval: _____

1   06

The following is a portion of the first report of the detective who was left alone by the other BPD officers on-scene about 10 a.m. that morning. The other officers were ordered to leave the Ramsey home and go back to the Boulder Police Department or off-shift. This report is from the morning of December 26, 1996, and continues through when JonBenét's body was found shortly after 1 p.m. that day. Detective Linda Arndt was the detective.

Arndt's report was turned in on January 8, 1997, thirteen days outside of the 24- to 48-hour universal deadline for detective reports on violent crime scenes. Arndt's report was therefore deemed to be a "recall" report by most district attorneys and would be actively questioned at a criminal trial.

Detective Supplemental Report: P96-21871
First degree murder
Det. Linda Arndt
Date of Report: January 8, 1997

On Dec. 26, 1996 at approx. 0635 hours I received a phone call at
my home phone number from Det. Sgt. Robert Whitson. Sgt. Whitson
informed me that officers were on the scene of a reported
kidnapping. The reported kidnapping had occurred at 755 15th St.
located in Boulder, Boulder County, Colorado. JonBenet Ramsey, a
6 year old female, was reported to have been kidnapped from her
home. JonBenet's mother had found a ransom letter inside the home
at approx. 0550 hours this morning. JonBenet had last been seen
inside her home at approx. 2200 hours on Dec. 25, 1996. There was
no apparent forced entry to the residence. Other family members
who were inside the home from the night of Dec. 25 through the
morning of Dec. 26 had not been harmed. These family members
included JonBenet's mother, father, and brother.

In the note left by the reported kidnappers, the author of the note
stated the reported kidnappers would phone the Ramseys between 0800
hours and 1000 hours. Sgt. Whitson requested that I respond to the
Ramsey address on 15th St. Sgt. Whitson was going to make attempts
to have US West Communications place a trace on all incoming calls
placed to the Ramsey home.

I went to the Boulder Police Dept. and obtained a hand held tape
recorder as well as my notebook. I met with Det. Fred Patterson at
the Boulder Police Dept. (BPD). Det. Patterson and I responded to
the Ramsey address located on 15th St. While at the BPD, I briefly
met with BPD Ofc. Karl Veitch. Ofc. Veitch informed me that he had
the ransom note which had been left by the reported kidnappers. I
requested that Ofc. Veitch make 3 copies of this note. This
request was carried out. I retained possession of one of the
copies of the note, another copy was given to Det. Patterson, and
the third copy was placed in a seal envelope and left on my desk.
I quickly reviewed the contents of this 3 page note. Det.
Patterson and I then responded to the Ramsey residence. Prior to
arriving at the residence we met with Watch III Sgt. Paul
Reichenbach. We met with Sgt. Reichenbach at the rear of the
Basemar shopping center at approx. 0755 hours. Sgt. Reichenbach
personally provided us with the following additional information:

    After officers had been dispatched to this call, all further
    communication was done by telephone rather than radio traffic.
    The first officer on the scene was Ofc. Rick French. Ofc.
    French had told Sgt. Reichenbach that something didn't seem
    right. The 6 year old daughter of John Ramsey, JonBenet
    Ramsey, had been kidnapped from her bedroom sometime between
    approx. 2200 hours on Dec. 25, 1996 and 0600 hours on Dec. 26,
    1996. A 2 1/2 page note had been found by JonBenet's mother.
    Demands in this note stated that $118,000 be paid to ensure
    the safe return of JonBenet. No police or law enforcement
    were to be notified, otherwise JonBenet would be

P96-21871   2

"decapitated."   The 2 1/2 page note had been found by
JonBenet's mother (Patsy Ramsey) at the bottom of a spiral
staircase located in the house.

John Ramsey is the president of Access Graphics.   This
business is located at 1426 Pearl St. in Boulder.   This
business is very successful.

Sgt. Reichenbach said there was a light dusting of snow on the
ground when he arrived at the Ramsey residence.   Sgt.
Reichenbach did not notice any footprints or other tracks in
the snow. Sgt. Reichenbach personally checked the exterior of
the Ramsey residence.   Sgt. Reichenbach did not notice any
signs of forced entry to the residence.

Sgt. Reichenbach had arranged through Boulder Regional
Communications Center (BRCC) dispatcher ██████████ to have a
trap placed on the Ramsey home phone number.   The home phone
number for the John Ramsey residence is (303) ████████.
Dispatcher ██████████ had spoken with ███████, an employee
with US West Communications.   The trap was activated and in
place by the time Det. Patterson and I arrived at the Ramsey
residence.   Sgt. Reichenbach informed me that US West
Communication would need a "letter of demand" on BPD
letterhead within 48 hours, explaining the necessity for this
trap.

Sgt. Reichenbach had informed us that Boulder County Sheriff's
Dept. (BCSD) Dep. Scott Williams was a canine officer.   Dep.
Williams was notified that his services may be needed, and was
placed on standby.   Sgt. Reichenbach also suggested that if a
bloodhound's services were needed, Aurora Police Dept. might
be able to assist.

Det. Patterson and I arrived at the Ramsey residence at approx.
0810 hours.   I personally met with BPD Ofc. Rick French.   Ofc.
French provided me with a synopsis of who was on the scene and what
had already been done.   BPD crime scene investigator Officers Barry
Weiss and Sue Barcklow were also at the Ramsey residence.   Ofc.
Weiss was photographing the interior and exterior of the residence.
Ofc. Barcklow was attempting to obtain latent fingerprints.   Areas
checked included: possible points of entry and exit to the
residence; as well as the spiral staircase leading from outside
JonBenet's bedroom to the first floor; and the door leading into
JonBenet's bedroom.   Ofc. French provided me with the following
information:

Ofc. French told me that when he arrived he met with Patsy
Ramsey, JonBenet's mother.   Patsy was very upset and
distraught and it was difficult for Ofc. French to obtain
information from her.   Ofc. French also spoke with John
Ramsey, JonBenet's father.   Ofc. French learned that the

1   19

P96-21871   3

Ramsey family had been at a friend's house on the late
afternoon and evening of Dec. 25, 1996. They returned home at
approx. 2200 hours on Dec. 25. JonBenet and her brother,
Burke, went to bed shortly after the family returned home.
John Ramsey had read to JonBenet after she'd gone to bed, and
before she went to sleep. JonBenet had last been seen wearing
a red turtleneck and white long underwear. Patsy woke up this
morning and discovered the suspected ransom note at the bottom
of the spiral staircase. Patsy originally thought that the
note may have been left by the housekeeper. Ofc. French had
been told that the Ramsey family had been planning to leave
early this morning for Michigan. The Ramsey family has a home
in upper Michigan. After Patsy discovered the note she went
to JonBenet's bedroom. Patsy discovered JonBenet was missing.

Ofc. French told me there was no apparent forced entry to the
Ramsey home. Ofc. French had checked the Ramsey home and had
not detected any sign of JonBenet. Four friends of the
Ramsey's had been notified by the Ramseys of JonBenet's
disappearance and were currently at the house. The pastor
from the Ramsey's church had also been notified and was also
present at the house. BPD Victim Advocates had been notified
and were also present inside the Ramsey home.

After I had briefly met with Ofc. French I met with John Ramsey.
I informed John Ramsey that US West Communications had already
placed a trap on incoming phone calls made to his home. I told Mr.
Ramsey that I would also like to connect a tape recorder to the
incoming phone line. John Ramsey gave me his verbal permission.
I asked John Ramsey for the location of the phones in the house, on
the first floor. John Ramsey showed me a telephone mounted on the
wall at the west end of the kitchen, and a telephone located in the
den. The den is located west of the kitchen. I connected the tape
recorder to the telephone located in the den. I informed Mr.
Ramsey that if the author of the suspected ransom note called, we
would be able to tape record the conversation. John Ramsey was
informed of my actions and gave his verbal consent. After the
phone recorder had been connected to the telephone in the den, I
instructed John Ramsey on the use of the tape recorder. John
Ramsey told me that he would answer the phone for all incoming
calls.

After the tape recorder had been connected to the telephone, I met
with Patsy Ramsey. Patsy was sitting on a chair in the sitting
room. This room is located at the southeast corner of the house on
the first floor. Two of Patsy's friends were with her, ██████,
██████, and ██████ ██████. Patsy spoke softly when she talked to
me. At times Patsy seemed to be staring off into the distance.
Patsy seemed to have a vacant look, and seemed dazed. Since Patsy
was situated in a room at some distance from the den, I had limited
contact with her. I asked Ofc. French to remain with Patsy. I did

P96-21871   4

ask Patsy a few questions and was able to receive some information.
The following is information I received from Patsy:

Patsy had gotten up on the morning of Dec. 26, 1996 and had
gone down the stairs from her bedroom to the kitchen. Patsy
used the back (i.e. west) stairway. The back stairway
consists of a spiral staircase leading from just outside
JonBenet's bedroom to the northwest corner of the first floor
of the house. At the bottom of this spiral staircase Patsy
discovered a 3 page handwritten note. The note had been
written on legal pad sized paper. Patsy said she originally
thought the note might have been left by her housekeeper.
After Patsy looked at the note and read it she ran to
JonBenet's bedroom. JonBenet was missing.

I asked Patsy who had keys to her home. Patsy said the woman
who was responsible for housekeeping at her home, ▓▓▓▓
▓▓▓▓▓▓, had a key to the home. I asked Patsy if the home had
an alarm system and if the alarm system had been activated on
the night of Dec. 25. Patsy told me that the home does have
an alarm system, however it had not been used for awhile.
Patsy did tell me that she believed the house had been locked
when she and the rest of her family went to bed on the night
of Dec. 25. Patsy said she had not received any suspicious
phone calls nor hang up phone calls in the past few weeks.
~~There had been no unwelcome solicitors nor suspicious persons~~
at the Ramsey home in the past few weeks.

Patsy said that she, her husband, JonBenet, and Berke (her 10
year old son) had planned on leaving Boulder on the morning of
Dec. 26. The family was going to fly to Michigan to spend
time at their summer home. I asked Patsy who knew about this
trip. Patsy said some of her close friends knew, and the
housekeeper knew. Patsy had not arranged for the neighbors or
anyone else to watch their home while the Ramsey family was in
Michigan.

I asked Patsy if she could think of anyone who might be
responsible for JonBenet's disappearance. Patsy told me that
her housekeeper, ▓▓▓▓▓▓▓▓▓, had asked to borrow money on
Dec. 24. Patsy told me that she had had a Christmas party at
her home on Dec. 23. ▓▓▓▓▓▓▓▓▓ was supposed to clean up
from this party on the morning of Dec. 24. Linda Hoffman had
phoned Patsy on the morning of Dec. 24. Linda Hoffman asked
Patsy if she could borrow some money. Patsy had said yes.
Patsy told me she had loaned money to ▓▓▓▓▓▓▓▓ in the
past. ▓▓▓▓▓▓▓▓▓▓ phoned Patsy again on the afternoon of
Dec. 24. ▓▓▓▓▓▓▓▓ was crying. ▓▓▓▓▓▓▓ said she
needed to borrow $2,000. Patsy thought the money was needed
for dental repair for ▓▓▓ and her family. Patsy told ▓▓▓
▓▓▓▓▓ that she would write a check for $2,000. Patsy said
she would leave the check on the kitchen counter. Patsy told

P96-21871   5

me that ███████████ was scheduled to be at the Ramsey home
on Friday morning, Dec. 27, at 0900 hours.

Patsy told me ███████████ has worked as her housekeeper for
about the past 2 years. ███████████ cleans the Ramsey home
twice a week. Ms ████ is paid $200 a week. Patsy told me
that Ms ███████ husband ███████████. Patsy
provided me with Ms ████ husband's name, ███████████.
Patsy also supplied me with Ms ███████████ home phone number,
███████████. Patsy further told me that Ms ████ adult
children have had problems in the past 2 months. Patsy
believed that one of Ms ███████ adult daughters had been in
contact with Safe House because of domestic violence problems.
Patsy did not know the name of this daughter, nor where she
lived. Patsy thought the daughter lived in ███████████, ██.
Patsy thought the adult daughter's domestic problems might
have occurred prior to Thanksgiving of 1996.

After I had spoken briefly with Patsy I returned to the den area of
the house. Each time the telephone rang I was present when John
Ramsey answered the phone. There were at least 3 times when John
Ramsey was not present in the den when the phone rang. I
personally saw John Ramsey run to the den to answer the phone. For
each incoming phone call received at the Ramsey home on the morning
of Dec. 26, John Ramsey told me that the caller was not associated
with the suspected ransom note.

While I was in the den the pastor from ███████████████████
Church in ███████ relayed a message to me. Patsy had told this
information to the pastor. I believe the pastor's first name was
███. The pastor told me about a telephone conversation Patsy had
had with her mother. Patsy's mother had spoken with the
housekeeper (███████████) while Patsy's mother had been living in
the Ramsey home. Ms ████████ had reportedly said that JonBenet was
so cute that someone would kidnap her. I met with Patsy and asked
her about her telephone conversation with her mother. Patsy told
me that she had spoken to her mother after she had discovered
JonBenet was missing. Patsy's mother is ███████████. ███████████
lives in Atlanta, GA. ███████████ had told Patsy that Ms ███████
had said "many times" that JonBenet was such a beautiful girl, and
wasn't ███████████ afraid that someone was going to kidnap her.
Patsy supplied me with ███████████ home phone number. This home
phone number is ███████████.

Det. Patterson was going to follow-up on information regarding Ms
████ and her family. Det. Patterson was going to attempt to
have US West Communications place a trace on Ms ███████ home
phone number.

Within about the first 20 minutes of arriving at the Ramsey
residence I asked John Ramsey if he would consent to having his
office telephones have a trap placed on them. John Ramsey did give

1 22

P96-21871   6

his verbal authorization. John Ramsey supplied me with the work
number for himself, as well as his first assistant. These phone
numbers were: ▮▮▮▮▮▮▮▮▮ and ▮▮▮▮▮▮▮▮▮, respectively.
Arrangements were made through US West to have a trap placed on
these two phone lines at Access Graphics.

There were 2 cellular phones at the Ramsey house when Det.
Patterson and I arrived. These cellular phones were used to make
phone calls from the Ramsey residence. The telephone at the Ramsey
house was not used to make outgoing phone calls on the morning of
Dec. 26. The cellular phones belonged to John Ramsey and ▮▮▮▮
▮. The friends who had been contacted by the Ramsey's, and
who were present with the Ramseys when I arrived, were: ▮▮▮▮ and
▮▮▮▮▮▮▮▮; ▮▮▮▮▮▮▮▮; and Pastor ▮▮ from ▮▮.
▮▮▮▮▮▮▮▮▮ Church in Boulder. Burke, the Ramsey's 9 year
old son, had already left the residence when I had arrived. Burke
was staying at the ▮▮▮ home located at ▮▮▮▮▮▮▮▮▮. in
Boulder.

After I had connected the tape recorder to the telephone, and had
briefly met with Patsy Ramsey, I talked with John Ramsey in the
den. I talked with John Ramsey about things to say when the
author(s) of the suspected ransom note called. I told John that he
should demand to talk to JonBenet. If John Ramsey was going to be
given instructions for meeting the purported kidnappers, I
instructed John Ramsey to obtain very specific instructions from
the caller. John Ramsey was told to say that he would not be able
to obtain the money until at least 1700 hours this date. I
supplied John Ramsey with a piece of note paper. I had John Ramsey
write notes on this piece of paper regarding what to say when the
author(s) of the suspected ransom note phoned. I retained this
notebook paper and later placed it into evidence (item 4LKA). The
third item written by John Ramsey was "must talk to JB." I had
placed an asterisk by this sentence.

▮▮▮▮▮▮▮▮, a friend of John Ramsey's, told John Ramsey that he
would be able to obtain the ransom amount from his bank. ▮▮▮▮
▮▮▮▮ left the Ramsey residence after I had arrived and met with
his banker. ▮▮▮▮▮▮▮▮ returned to the Ramsey residence prior to
about 0930 hours. ▮▮▮▮▮▮▮▮ told me that he had arranged with
his banker to have $118,000 in cash be available. This amount was
available when ▮▮▮▮▮▮▮ returned to the Ramsey residence. The
amount had been arranged in the denominations demanded in the
suspected ransom note. ▮▮▮▮▮▮▮ told me he was able to get this
amount obtained within approx. one hour of notifying his banker.
▮▮▮▮▮▮▮▮ told me that $118,000 is a relatively insignificant
amount compared to John Ramsey's wealth. ▮▮▮▮▮▮▮ told me that
the persons who demanded the ransom could easily have asked for
$10,000,000 and had obtained that amount.

Prior to 1000 hours I remained in, or near, the den area of the
house. Patsy Ramsey remained in the front sitting room area. The

friends of the Ramsey's and the pastor divided their time between
Patsy and John. John Ramsey paced between the area of the den and
the formal dining room. John was usually by himself. I did not
see John or Patsy interact with each other. No one in the house
made any obvious comment to me that it was after 1000 hours and the
suspected kidnappers had not called. From the time I arrived at
the Ramsey house until approx. 1000 hours I had a few brief
conversations with John. I had asked John if the doors to the
house had been locked when the family went to bed last night. John
told me that he personally checked all of the doors and all of the
windows in the home this morning. All of the doors and windows
were locked. John told me that although the house does have an
alarm system, the family has not used the alarm system for months.
I asked John who had keys to the residence. John told me his adult
son has a key to the house. The son had been in Atlanta since Dec.
15, 1996. The adult son, John Andrew, had been attending college
at the University of Colorado - Boulder. Another family member,
Patsy's mother, also had a key to the residence. Patsy's mother is
currently living in Atlanta, GA. I asked John if any keys had been
hidden outside the house. John told me there were no hidden keys.
I asked John of any keys had been lost or stolen. John told me
there had been no stolen or lost house keys. John told me that the
housekeeper, ▇▇▇▇▇▇▇▇▇▇, did have a key to the house. ▇▇▇▇
▇▇▇▇▇▇ was the only person living in Colorado who had a key to the
Ramsey house.

John Ramsey told me that he and his family had been at a dinner
party held at the ▇▇▇▇▇▇▇▇ home on the afternoon and evening of
Dec. 25, 1996. John, Patsy, Burke, and JonBenet had returned home
at approx. 2200 hours. John told me that Patsy and Burke
immediately went to bed. John had read a book to JonBenet, tucked
her into bed, then John went to bed. John said he went to bed at
approx. 2230 hours.

John told me that he is the President and CEO of Access Graphics.
There was an article in the Boulder Daily Camera newspaper within
this past month about Access Graphics. The news article had been
written because Access Graphics had just grossed over
$1,000,000,000. John told me that Access Graphics has over 300
employees. John told me that Access Graphics resulted from a
merger of 3 businesses in the mid-1980s. John Ramsey had been the
founder of one of these businesses. John's business had been in
Atlanta, GA at the time. John informed me that Access Graphics has
business offices located in Mexico City, Mexico and Amsterdam.

I asked John if he could think of any past, or current, employee of
Access Graphics who might be responsible for the disappearance of
JonBenet. John told me he was not directly responsible for hiring
or firing. John talked about the employees at Access Graphics as
being all part of a family. John did tell me that there was one
employee that he was forced to "let go" approx. 5 months ago. The
name of this employee is ▇▇▇▇▇▇▇. John said that ▇▇▇ and his

8

P96-21871

wife, ███████████, are currently living in ███████████, CO. John told me he had not seen ███████ since ███████ left the company. John told me he could not think of anyone with whom he had disagreement with.

I asked John which interior lights, if any, were on when he went to bed on the night of Dec. 25. John told me no interior lights were on when he went to bed. I asked John which exterior lights were on when he went to bed. John told me that he didn't know if any exterior lights were on. John said the Christmas lights located in the front of the house may have been left on, and possibly an exterior light. There are small white Christmas lights lining the sides of the sidewalk extending toward the front of the house. These Christmas lights were on when I first arrived at the Ramsey residence.

After ███████████ had been named as a possible suspect, I asked John if he had any photos of ███████████ in the house. John Ramsey told me that he had a roll of film in his camera. Pictures had been taken of the Christmas party held at the Ramsey home on Dec. 23. John told me that ███████████ had attended that party. I asked John for the film from that camera. John personally provided me with the film from that camera. I gave the roll of 35 mm film to Ofc. Barry Weiss. I instructed Ofc. Weiss to have the file developed ASAP. I asked John if he had any paperwork in the house which might contain ███████████ handwriting. John checked the kitchen area for any note, but did not locate any. I asked John if he had cancelled checks which had been endorsed by ███████████. John phoned his bank. John was told that the bank did have copies of checks which had been written to, and endorsed by, ███████████. I asked John to have his bank fax those checks to me in care of the fax number located at the BPD Detective Bureau. This fax number is (303) ███████████.

I asked John and Patsy for current photos of JonBenet. I explained that the photos would be copied and distributed to local law enforcement agencies. I was given two 8x10 photographs of JonBenet as well as and 8x10 portfolio of JonBenet containing 2 pictures and her physical description. I gave these photos to Ofc. Barry Weiss and instructed him to have copies made and to relay the copies to Sgt. Larry Mason at the Boulder Police Dept. Ofc. Weiss and Ofc. Barcklow cleared the Ramsey residence at approx. 1015 hours.

At an unknown time between approx. 0900 hours and 0945 hours Det. Sgt. Robert Whitson arrived at the Ramsey residence. Sgt. Whitson talked with John Ramsey in the den area of the house. I was present during part of this conversation. Sgt. Whitson informed John Ramsey that the FBI had been notified and was assisting in this investigation. Sgt. Whitson told John Ramsey that we would need a sample of his handwriting. John verbally agreed to supply Sgt. Whitson with a handwriting sample. Shortly after Sgt. Whitson had requested this sample, John Ramsey wrote and line on a legal

P96-21871   9

pad in front of him and signed his name to this pad. I was sitting
next to John Ramsey when he wrote this. John has written "Now is
the time for all people," then signed his name. I removed this
sheet of paper from the legal pad, secured it in my notebook, and
later placed it into evidence (item 4LKA).

Before Ofc. Barry Weiss left, I asked him to show me what areas of
the house he had processed for evidence. The first floor glass
door located on the north side of the house, east of the spiral
staircase, had been processed for latent fingerprints. John Ramsey
had told me that this was the only door in the house that did not
have a dead bolt to secure it. The spiral staircase located at the
northwest corner of the house, extending from the first floor to
the second floor, was processed for latent fingerprints. There was
a green Christmas garland covering the handrail portion of this
staircase. At the top of the spiral staircase was an open laundry
area. JonBenet's bedroom door was located south of this laundry
area. Ofc. Weiss walked to the patio door located at the south end
of JonBenet's bedroom. Ofc. Weiss told me that there had been
frost on the patio when officers had arrived. The frost had not
been disturbed. Det. Patterson had entered JonBenet's bedroom. I
walked into JonBenet's bedroom, only as far as the first bed. I
did not touch anything. Ofc. Weiss pointed out a bedroom located
west of JonBenet's bedroom. I entered into this bedroom a few
steps, but did not touch anything. Ofc. Weiss then walked east
along the second floor hallway into the children's playroom area.
I noticed that there was a life size Barbie doll standing next to
the north window. The doll was not clothed. Continuing east down
this hallway there is a bathroom located on the north side of the
hallway and a smaller bedroom located across from this bathroom.
At the east end of the hallway is Burke's bedroom. Outside of
Burke's bedroom is a stairway leading upstairs to the master
bedroom. The stairway also leads downstairs to the front door. I
walked upstairs into the master bedroom. I did not touch anything
in the master bedroom area. I returned to the second floor using
the west steps. The west steps enter the second floor area just
east of JonBenet's bedroom, and just east of the open laundry area.

Sgt. Whitson requested that the door to JonBenet's room be sealed.
Prior to his arrival, the door to JonBenet's room had been closed
but not locked. I obtained a police crime scene tape and adhesive
tape from Sgt. Whitson's vehicle. Det. Patterson and I sealed the
entrance to JonBenet's room at approx. 1030 hours. At approx. 1035
hours all BPD officers, detectives, and victim advocates cleared
the Ramsey residence. The only persons remaining in the residence
were: John Ramsey, Patsy Ramsey, ███████, ███████,
███████, ███████, ███████, and myself.

I talked with John briefly after all of the officers had left.
John told me that he and Patsy had been married 16 to 17 years.
Patsy had been diagnosed with ovarian cancer 3 years ago. Patsy
recently discovered that she was free of cancer. John's adult

P96-21871   10

daughter had been killed in a car accident 4 years ago.   I asked
John if there had been any suspicious people at his residence
within the last few weeks.   John told me no.   I asked John if he
had received any suspicious phone calls or hang up phone calls
within the last few weeks.   John told me no.

John Ramsey, ███████████, ███████████, ███████████, and I were in
the den area talking at an unknown time after 1040 hours.   I had
placed my copy of the suspected ransom note on the table in the den
and had asked John to review the note.   I had asked John Ramsey to
tell me what unusual things he detected from reading the note.
John Ramsey said very little.   John Ramsey's friends asked me my
opinion of the note.   I told John Ramsey's friends that the note
appeared to be directed towards John Ramsey.   The note also
appeared to be personal, as it referred to John Ramsey as "John"
throughout the note.   John Ramsey's friends made the following
observations about the note: The author of the note directed the
note to John Ramsey; the amount of $118,000 was an odd amount; the
author of the note appeared to be somewhat educated, since the
words "hence" and "attache" were used; the sentence "don't try to
grow a brain John" seemed to be a slap in the face to John Ramsey;
the closure "Victory!   S.B.T.C." did not make sense; and the
reference to John Ramsey being a southerner indicated to the
friends the person did not really know John Ramsey because John was
originally from Michigan.   I asked John Ramsey if he had given a
loan to anyone in the amount of $118,000.   John said he had not.
I asked John if he owed $118,000.   John said he did not.

At an unknown time between approx. 1040 hours and 1200 hours John
Ramsey left the house and picked up the family's mail.   I was not
present when John left.   I did witness John Ramsey opening his mail
in the kitchen.   ███████████ also left the Ramsey home.   ████ left
sometime after 1015 hours.   ████ told me he had also taken photos
of the Christmas party held at the Ramsey's home on Dec. 23.   ████
left to have his film developed at a one-hour photo lab.   ████
returned within about 30 minutes to an hour.   At approx. noon Patsy
relocated to the den area.   Patsy laid down on the couch in the
den.   ███████████ remained with Patsy.   ███████████ also
stayed with Patsy.   ███████████, ███████████, and John
Ramsey were in the kitchen area and formal dining room area of the
house.   Patsy asked me what we (i.e. police) were doing.   I told
Patsy that we were attempting to locate ███████████.   I also told
Patsy that the FBI was involved in this investigation.   Patsy had
asked me these questions when I initially spoke with her.   Patsy
talked with me about the suspected ransom note.   Patsy told me that
███████████ did not use the language contained within the note.
Patsy explained to me that ███████████ did not use the words
"hence" or "attache" case.   Patsy did not know why someone would
ask for the amount of $118,000.   Patsy said that amount had no
significance to her.   Patsy asked me why the author of the note had
not asked for a larger sum of money, or at least a round sum of
money.   Patsy said the author of the note referred to John as being

P96-21871   11

a Southerner. Patsy told me that anyone who knows John Ramsey
knows he's not from the South. I asked Patsy when ████████
was next scheduled to be at their home. ████████████ was due to
be at the Ramsey home at 0900 hours on Friday, Dec. 27. While I
was talking to Patsy she would repeatedly start crying. Patsy
would be unable to speak. Patsy repeatedly asked "why didn't I
hear my baby?" Patsy looked physically exhausted. Patsy would
close her eyes, but was not able to rest or sleep.

When I talked briefly with John Ramsey during the morning of Dec.
26 he was able to carry on a conversation and articulate his words.
John Ramsey had smiled, joked, and seemed to focus during the
conversation. Patsy seemed to be much less focused when I spoke
with her. Patsy seemed to have a far-off look in her expression.
Patsy's thoughts were scattered and it was difficult to get her to
stay focused on one thought. Patsy would collapse in tears and
repeatedly asked why had she not been able to hear her baby. There
were 2 phone calls received by John Ramsey when I saw him act
differently than he had all morning. When he received each of
these phone calls, John stood in front of the north door located
between the den and the kitchen. John looked outside during the
phone call. John told the caller that JonBenet had been
"kidnapped." John was sobbing and had difficulty speaking. At
times, John was unable to speak. I was told by friends the
identity of the 2 callers. One caller was John Ramsey's son, John
Andrew Ramsey. The other caller was John Ramsey's daughter,
Melinda Ramsey. John Ramsey told me that his Boulder family was
planning on flying to Michigan this morning. John's adult children
from another marriage, John Andrew and Melinda, had taken the
family's private plane from Atlanta and had flown to Minneapolis,
MN. John Ramsey, Patsy, JonBenet, and Burke were going to fly to
Minneapolis, MN and meet with John Andrew and Melinda. The 6
Ramseys were then going to fly to their summer home located in
Charlevoix, MI. They were going to return to Boulder on Sunday,
Dec. 29.

At approx. noon I paged Det. Sgt. Mason and asked that he phone me
at the cellular phone number for one of the phones at the Ramsey
house. Patsy Ramsey had been repeatedly asking me for an update.
At approx. 1230 hours I again paged Det. Sgt. Mason and asked him
to phone me. I did not receive a call from either of these pages.
At approx. 1230 hours I noticed that John Ramsey seemed to be by
himself. John Ramsey was alone in the formal dining room area of
the house. John Ramsey seemed to isolate himself from others.
Earlier in the morning, I noticed that when John Ramsey was sitting
down, he would look down and his leg would be bouncing. At an
unknown time between 1230 hours and 1300 hours I talked with ████
████. I told ██████ that I needed his help to keep John Ramsey's
mind occupied. I suggested to ████████████ that he and John Ramsey
check the house "from top to bottom," excluding JonBenet's bedroom.
I suggested to ██████ that John Ramsey check to see if anything
belonging to JonBenet had been taken or left behind. ██████ told me

P96-21871   12

that he had reported his daughter missing to the Boulder Police
Dept. this past year. ████ had checked the house and found his
daughter inside the house. ████ said his daughter had been
hiding. ████ told me it was hard for him at that time not to be
able to do anything. I then spoke to John Ramsey. I suggested to
John Ramsey that he and ████████ check the house "from top to
bottom" to see if anything belonging to JonBenet had been taken or
had been left behind. I talked with John Ramsey in the kitchen of
the house. After I had spoken to John he immediately went to the
basement door. I saw ████ following John Ramsey. I then returned
to the den area. The time was approx. 1300 hours.

At approx. 1301 hours I received a page to phone BPD number ██-
██. There was no answer. I had tried to make this call using
one of the cellular phones at the house. I then returned to the
den. At approx. 1305 hours I saw ███████ run from the area of
the basement door to the den. I heard some type of shout or scream
before I saw ████. I saw ████ grab the phone in the den, dial 2
to 3 numbers, then hang up the phone. ████ then ran back towards
the basement door. ████ yelled for someone to call an ambulance.
I followed ████ to the basement door. The door to the basement
was wide open. I was standing in the hallway, facing the door to
the basement, when I saw John Ramsey coming up the final three or
four stairs. John was carrying a young girl in his arms. The
young girl had long blonde hair. John Ramsey was carrying the
young girl in front of him, using both of his arms to hold her
around her waist area. The young girl's head was above John
Ramsey's head while he was carrying her. From a distance of
approx. 3 feet, as John was walking up the stairs, I was able to
make the following observations to this young girl: both of her
arms were raised above her head and were motionless; her lips
appeared blue; her body appeared to have rigor mortis; there was a
white string attached to her right wrist; there was a bright red
mark, approx. the size of a quarter, at the front of her neck; the
lower portion of her neck and the right side of her face appeared
to have livor mortis. I told John to place the young girl's body
on the rug just inside the front doorway. John did as he was
instructed. The young girl was JonBenet. JonBenet appeared to
have been dead for a period of time. I touched JonBenet's neck in
an attempt to locate any sign that she was alive. JonBenet's skin
was cool to the touch. There was dried mucus from one of
JonBenet's nostrils. My face was within inches of JonBenet's face.
I detected an odor of decay. John Ramsey asked me if JonBenet was
alive. I don't remember the specific words John Ramsey used. I
told John Ramsey that his daughter was dead. John Ramsey moaned.
I told John Ramsey to go back to the den, where the other persons
in the house were congregated. I told John Ramsey to phone 911 and
have detectives and a coroner respond. I told John Ramsey to go to
Patsy.

After John Ramsey left I picked up JonBenet and carried her into
the living room. I laid JonBenet on the rug located inside the

P96-21871   13

living room. I noticed that JonBenet was wearing long white cotton
pajama-like pants. JonBenet was also wearing a long sleeved white
cotton or knit top. JonBenet's face was turned to her right side.
There were no coverings on JonBenet's feet. JonBenet's feet
appeared to be white (i.e. drained of color). I did not notice any
marks to her feet. Shortly after I had moved JonBenet into the
living room I heard a loud guttural moan and wail coming from the
den area of the house. The noise sounded as though it was made by
a woman.

John Ramsey came into the living room area approx. 1 to 2 minutes
after I had sent him back to the den. As John entered the room he
asked me if he could cover up JonBenet. John grabbed a throw
blanket that was lying on a chair located immediately inside the
living room. John placed this blanket over JonBenet's body before
I had a chance to speak. I adjusted the blanket on JonBenet's body
so that her clothing was covered from her neck down. I also
covered the neck area of JonBenet. I had covered the wound on
JonBenet's neck with her long sleeved shirt before John Ramsey
arrived in the living room. I told John Ramsey that he could say
good-bye to his daughter, but he could not move her body, touch her
hands, or lower the blanket. John knelt on the floor next to
JonBenet. John repeatedly referred to JonBenet as "my little
angel." John stroked JonBenet's hair with one of his hands. John
Ramsey laid down next to JonBenet, placed an arm around her body,
and made sounds as though he was crying. I did not notice any
tears. John Ramsey then rolled away from JonBenet's body and went
into a kneeling position. When John rolled away from JonBenet's
body he looked around, towards the hallway. John Ramsey then knelt
by JonBenet's body, hugged her, and called her his little angel.
After approx. 5 to 10 seconds John stopped hugging JonBenet and
again looked toward the hallway. John remained kneeling near
JonBenet when I looked into the hallway, towards the den. I was
able to watch JonBenet, John Ramsey, and the people coming from the
den toward the living room. I saw Patsy Ramsey. It seemed as
though Patsy was unable to walk without the assistance of someone
on each side of her, holding her up. ████████, Patsy, ████
█, ████████████, ████████████, and ████████ all came
into the living room area. When Patsy saw JonBenet's body she
immediately went to her and laid on top of her. As I faced
JonBenet from the hallway, John Ramsey was to the right of her
body, ███████ was near JonBenet's head, Patsy Ramsey was next to
█, ████████████ was next to Patsy (near JonBenet's
feet), and ████████ and ████████████ were also near the lower
portion of JonBenet's body. ████████ left the living room and
went into the kitchen area. ████████ seemed to be very upset. When
████████████ entered the living room, she was shaking and her
eyes were wide. ████████ grabbed onto my arm and repeatedly told me
not to leave. I asked ████████ to pray for JonBenet and to lead
everyone in a prayer. I then stood near the piano in the living
room and was able to watch everyone in the living room, as well as
████████, who was still in the kitchen area.

P96-21871   14

Patsy was crying and moaning while she was with JonBenet.   Patsy
raised herself onto her knees, lifted her arms straight into the
air, and prayed.   Patsy said "Jesus! You raised Lazarus from the
dead, raise my baby from the dead!" At approx. 1312 hours there
had been no officer response. There had also been no response from
the coroner or an ambulance.   The closest phone was a cellular
phone in the kitchen. This phone was located approx. 12 feet away.
I quickly walked into the kitchen, grabbed the cellular phone, and
returned to the area in the hallway right outside the living room.
I phoned 911.   I reached Dispatcher Santiago.   I told the
dispatcher that I needed a detective response and a coroner at my
location.   I identified myself by my radio number, 156.   Within
approx. 3 to 5 minutes of this 911 phone call I made a second 911
phone call.   I again reached a dispatcher whose voice I did not
recognize. I was transferred to a supervisor. I informed the male
supervisor that I needed detective response, the coroner, and an
ambulance at my present location.   I gave my location as 755 15th
St. I told the dispatcher that I was at the scene of a homicide.
Prior to making this second 911 phone call I had seen an ambulance
drive slowly northbound on 15th St., past the Ramsey residence. At
approx. 1320 or 1325 hours Ofc. Barry Weiss arrived at the Ramsey
residence. Ofc. Weiss had responded to the first floor north door,
located off the caterer's kitchen. Ofc. Weiss had been calling out
my name.   I briefly met with Ofc. Weiss and then returned to the
hallway outside the living room area. I informed Ofc. Weiss of the
current situation.

At an unknown time after JonBenet's body was found, and prior to
Ofc. Weiss' arrival, I instructed ████████ to stand guard in
front of the basement door. I told ████ that no one was to enter
the basement area.   After Ofc. Weiss arrived I met with the
following BPD officers: Watch I Sgt. Dave Kicera, Ofc. Alaric
Morgan, Ofc. Rick French, Det. Bill Palmer, and Sgt. Larry Mason.
Agent Ron Walker with the FBI had accompanied Sgt. Mason.
Paramedics from AMR Ambulance also arrived.   After Ofc. Weiss
arrived I had requested that an ambulance respond. Patsy Ramsey
appeared to be swooning and I was concerned for her health.   The
paramedics did physically check Patsy Ramsey. The paramedics did
not examine nor touch JonBenet.   I was told that Patsy Ramsey was
obviously very distraught, however she physically did not need to
have medical attention. The two paramedics cleared the scene after
Patsy was checked.

At 1315 hours I received a page from communications.   The page
stated that Sgt. Kicera was at the front door at 875 15th St. Sgt.
Kicera was unable to find me.   I also received a page on my pager
at approx. 1329 hours. The page stated that my cellular 911 call
had been received by Weld County. Weld County Communications did
not understand me. I was instructed to call Boulder Communications
Center if I needed assistance.

After BPD officers arrived everyone was cleared out of the living

P96-21871   15

room. JonBenet's body was left where I had placed her. At approx.
1340 hours Det. Bill Palmer told me that he overheard a phone
conversation made by John Ramsey.   John Ramsey was making
arrangements to fly to Atlanta either that afternoon or that
evening.

Arrangements were made for John and Patsy Ramsey, ████████
█████████, ██████████, and ███████████████ to go to
the ████ residence. The ████████ live at ████████████ in
Boulder. At approx. 1400 hours I received a page to phone Det.
Patterson.   I phoned Det. Patterson using one of the cellular
phones in the kitchen. Det. Patterson told me that he was going to
attempt to contact and interview Burke Ramsey.   Det. Patterson
asked where Burke was staying. I informed Det. Patterson Burke was
at the ████████████ residence located at ████████████
█████ in Boulder. ████████████ family members were watching Burke.
One of the family members at the house was ██████████████.

I cleared the Ramsey residence at approx. 1435 hours.   The Ramsey
residence was vacated after John and Patsy Ramsey and their friends
had left the residence. Officers cleared the residence and awaited
a search warrant before returning.   John Ramsey had been wearing
khaki pants and a blue and white long sleeved striped shirt when I
had last seen him. Det. Patterson told me that he was going to
a red turtleneck sweater when I had last seen her. There had been
a paperbag containing children's clothing which was sitting in the
doorway to the den throughout most of the morning. After approx.
11 a.m. I moved the bag to the cloak room area, which is located
next to the door leading into the garage. ████████████ told me
the clothing contained outer clothing for JonBenet and Burke.
Winter ski pants, two winter jackets, and boots had been contained
within this bag. ██████████ removed these items and placed them in
the cloak room area.

When I had asked about doors being locked in the house, John Ramsey
told me that the door leading from the garage into the house is
always left unlocked. John further told me that the garage area is
always secured from the outside.   Before Ofc. Weiss left the
residence on the morning of Dec. 26, I believe he opened the door
leading from the house into the garage area.   I briefly saw a
utility vehicle and a car. Ofc. Weiss told me that the car was a
Jaguar.

After I had cleared the Ramsey residence I returned to the Boulder
Police Dept.   I met with Det. James Byfield and assisted him in
completing a search warrant for the Ramsey residence.   I also
attended a general detective briefing.

When John Ramsey met with me in the living room, after JonBenet's
body had been found, I asked him where he had found JonBenet. John
Ramsey told me JonBenet had been in the wine cellar. John Ramsey
told me JonBenet had been lying underneath a blanket. John told me

that JonBenet's arms had been tied. JonBenet had a piece of tape covering her mouth. John told me he removed the tape from JonBenet's mouth. John said he then grabbed JonBenet and carried her upstairs. One of the first things John told me after he came into the living room and had covered JonBenet's body was, "It has to be an inside job." John told me I was right, it had to be someone who knew the family. John told me that no one knows about the wine cellar in the basement, and therefore it had to be an inside job.

Ofc. French briefly talked with me at the Ramsey residence after JonBenet's body had been found. Ofc. French asked where JonBenet's body had been discovered. I told Ofc. French that John Ramsey said JonBenet had been found in the wine cellar in the basement. Ofc. French asked me to describe this room. I had not been downstairs and could not describe it. Ofc. French told me that when he did check the house, he checked the basement area. Ofc. French had not checked behind one door in the basement. This door had a latch on the top frame of the door. The door was latched. I briefly talked with ████████ after officers arrived at the Ramsey residence (after JonBenet's body had been found). I asked ████ where he was when JonBenet's body was found. ████ told me he was a few steps behind John Ramsey. John Ramsey had entered the wine cellar room located in the basement of the house. ████████ was not able to see inside the room because his vision was blocked by the door. ████ heard John Ramsey cry out.

I obtained the following information from the general detective briefing held on the late afternoon of Dec. 26:

Det. Patterson had conducted an interview with Burke Ramsey. Burke Ramsey said he and the three other members of his family had attended a party held at the ████████ residence on Dec. 25, 1996. The Ramseys were at the dinner party from approx. 1630 hours until 2100 to 2130 hours. Crab was served at this dinner. John and Patsy Ramsey disciplined each of their children by talking to them. John and Patsy Ramsey do not use any corporal punishment on their children. Burke said there had been no family arguments prior to, nor on, Dec. 25.
Det. Idler talked with the houseguests who were staying at ████████ home. The houseguests told Det. Idler that John and Patsy Ramsey treat each of their children fairly. One of the houseguests did say that Patsy adored JonBenet. Det. Idler was told that an adult daughter of John Ramsey's, from a previous marriage, had been killed in a car accident approx. 5 years ago. Det. Idler had also been told that Patsy Ramsey had been diagnosed with ovarian cancer. Patsy had recovered from the cancer approx. 2 years ago. Det. Idler was told that John and Patsy Ramsey had held a Christmas party at their home on Dec. 23. Extra caterers had been hired to assist with this party.

P96-21871   17

John Ramsey had told me that he and Patsy had hosted a Christmas party at their home for their children's friends. I thought John Ramsey told me this open house had been held on Dec. 24. The children who attended the party had decorated gingerbread houses. The gingerbread houses decorated by JonBenet and by Burke had been sitting on the dining room table located just south of the kitchen in the Ramsey residence. John Ramsey told me this information after I had asked him about those two gingerbread houses. ███████████ had also talked with me about the gingerbread houses. ██████████ had told me that Patsy Ramsey was the only woman she know who would allow young children to decorate their own gingerbread houses. ████████ children ███████ and ████████ had also attended this Christmas gathering.

Det. Idler had spoken with ████████. ████ told Det. Idler that he had searched the Ramsey house after he had arrived at the Ramsey residence earlier this morning. ████ said he had opened the door to the wine cellar. ████ was unable to locate a light switch for the wine cellar. ████ did not enter the wine cellar. ████ had said the interior of the wine cellar was dark and he did not see anything inside. ████ said the latch to the wine cellar, located at the top of the door, was secured when he checked it. ████ re-secured the latch to the wine cellar after he closed the door.

The search warrant prepared by Det. Byfield was signed by Boulder County Judge Diane MacDonald on the early evening of Dec. 26, 1996. I was notified that the search warrant had been signed at approx. 2000 hours. I responded to the Ramsey residence. Det. Barry Hartkopp and I used crime scene tape and secured the exterior property of the Ramsey residence with this tape. The crime scene tape was placed along the south, east, and north borders of the Ramsey property. The crime scene tape was also attached to the two wooden fences located on either side of the driveway located at the rear (west) of the residence, and along side the alley. BPD officers had been positioned in the alley located in the rear of the residence, and also at the front of the residence, to ensure the security of the house.

The Boulder County Coroner, Dr. John Meyers, was the first person to enter the Ramsey residence after the search warrant had been obtained. Dr. Meyers entered the Ramsey residence at approx. 2023 hours. Dr. Meyers entered through the front door. Dr. Meyers placed protective booties on each of his feet before he entered the residence. Dr. Meyers also covered his hands with plastic gloves before entering the residence. Dr. Meyers was told the location of JonBenet's body. Dr. Meyers exited the residence through the front door. Dr. Meyers told me he had examined JonBenet's body. Dr. Meyers pronounced JonBenet dead. Dr. Meyers told me he had observed ligature marks on JonBenet's neck. Dr. Meyers had noted petechial hemorrhage to JonBenet's eyes. Based on my training and experience, it is my experience that petechial hemorrhage to the

The following is a BPD report from Detective Linda Arndt from Friday, December 27, 1996.

John Ramsey had asked if the BPD would send some officers by so he could talk with them. Arndt and another officer, Sergeant Larry Mason, responded.

P96-21871   8

given.   Dr. Meyer invited Dr. Sirotnak to examine JonBenet,
particularly the trauma to JonBenet's vaginal area. Dr. Sirotnak
did conduct an examination on JonBenet after the conclusion of this
meeting.   Det. Trujillo was going to be present for this
examination.

At approx. 2130 hours Det. Sgt. Larry Mason and I met with John
Ramsey at the ██████ residence. Sgt. Mason and I met with John
Ramsey in an office area room located in the basement of the ██████
residence.   Other persons present in this room included: John
Ramsey's brother, Jeff Ramsey; ███████████, who introduced
himself as an attorney and a stockbroker with██████████ located
in Atlanta, GA; Dr. ██████, the physician for the Ramsey family; and
Mike Bynum, who described himself as a friend of John Ramsey and
also as an attorney who was providing John Ramsey with advice.
Sgt. Mason and I met with John Ramsey for approx. 40 minutes. The
following information was learned from this meeting:

I asked to speak with Patsy Ramsey. I was told by Dr. ██████
that Patsy Ramsey was too medicated to talk to anyone. Dr.
██████ had given Patsy valium.

John was told that there was a broken window located in the
basement of his home. John told us that he had broken out a
basement window approx. 4 to 5 months ago. This window was
located in the room where the Christmas decorations were kept.
The grate covering the window well to this window was not
secured. John had been locked out of the house. John told us
he removed the grate, kicked in the basement window, and
gained entrance to the house from this window. John told us
he had not re-secured the window nor had he fixed the window
which he had broken.

Sgt. Mason had told John it would be helpful to our
investigation if we could interview he and Patsy as soon as
possible. Sgt. Mason requested that we interview John and
Patsy on Saturday morning, Dec. 28. Dr. Beuff told Sgt. Mason
he did not know if Patsy would be available for an interview
at that time. Dr. Beuff said that Patsy was in a fragile
emotional state and he did not want to subject her to anything
which would further upset her. No definite answer was given
regarding the request to interview John.

I again asked John if he could think of anyone who might be a
possible suspect in this investigation. John told me that he
could only think of two persons from Access Graphics who might
be considered a suspect. John had previously given me the
name of one of these individuals, ██████. The other
person was a man who had been fired from Access Graphics
approx. 3 years ago. John told me that he had talked to the
person in charge of Human Resources at Access Graphics. John
had asked if potential employees could be asked the question

P96-21871   9

of whether or not they smoked. John was told this question
could be asked. The male employee was asked this question.
The male employee stated that he was not a smoker. After the
male employee was hired it was discovered that he was a
smoker. John said the man was fired because he had lied on
his application, not because he was a smoker. The man sued
Access Graphics. The lawsuit was reported in the local
newspaper. John told me that the lawsuit was settled. The
former employee received a $15,000 settlement. John said he
had not received any contact from this employee after the
lawsuit had been settled.

John told us that this was a difficult time of year for him.
John told me that his daughter, Beth, had been killed in a car
accident on Jan. 8, 1992. John also told me that this was a
difficult time for Patsy. Patsy had been diagnosed with
ovarian cancer two years ago. Patsy had undergone treatment
and the cancer had been removed.

John Ramsey told us that he was thinking about offering a
reward. John did not ask any questions about the results of
JonBenet's autopsy. John told us that there would be a
private memorial service for JonBenet at St. John's
Presbyterian Church in Boulder on Sunday afternoon. The
memorial service would be held at 1400 hours. The memorial
service was not open to the public. After the conclusion of
the memorial service John and his family would be flying to
Atlanta, GA. JonBenet's funeral was to be held on Tuesday,
Dec. 31, in Atlanta, GA. JonBenet was going to be buried next
to her half-sister, Beth Ramsey. When Sgt. Mason and I left
John we told him we would phone him in the morning to arrange
for interviews for he and Patsy.

End of Report.

cln

1 12

This is a report from the other detective who originally responded to the scene with Detective Arndt. Detective Fred Patterson left at approximately 9:45 to accompany Commander-Sergeant Bob Whitson back to the police department to debrief the FBI and other officers who were just arriving. This is the part of Patterson's report that deals with the morning of December 26, 1996.

Patterson

PCR P96-21871
Page 4

accompany Sgt. Whitson back to the police department for a briefing. Prior to leaving Sgt. Whitson asked that I attempt to obtain handwriting samples from John and Patsy Ramsey. I spoke with John Ramsey about the handwriting samples. He went out of the den to a counter near the bottom of the spiral staircase. He picked up two letter sized pads of white lined paper and handed them to me. He said that one was Patsy's and one was his that they used to write messages on. I identified each pad with the name of the person he identified as the writer and then gave the pads to Sgt. Whitson for later comparison with the ransom note. Sgt. Whitson maintained custody of the pads.

Sgt. Whitson and I then left the residence to return to the police department. We went to his vehicle and then drove around the neighbor. I used his video camera to tape vehicles that were in the area in a two-block radius of the residence. This had been suggested to Sgt. Whitson by the FBI. After completing the taping we returned to the police department.

At the police department, I contacted Det Chrisp and determined no further activity had occurred at the ████ residence. He said he would continue checking periodically.

I then attended a briefing at the police department. During the briefing I was supplied the name of ████ as the contact person at U.S. West for the trap/trace information. I also was advised that Legal Advisor Keatley was working on the affidavit for the court order based on the information I had provided. During the briefing we were advised that the body of JonBenet Ramsey was found in the house at 755 15th street in the basement.

After the briefing I met with Keatley and supplied him with the complete information he needed. He was working with U.S. West for the necessary information for the cover sheet. Keatley advised the affidavit would be ready to take to the judge later in the day.

Det. Idler and I were then assigned to go to ████ in Boulder and interview Burke Ramsey, the nine-year old son of Patsy and John Ramsey, about the kidnaping. We drove to that location and contacted several people at the residence. I conducted a taped interview with Burke Ramsey in an upstairs bedroom of the residence. ████ was present during the interview. She was the person watching Burke at the White's residence. Det. Idler conducted interviews with the other parties present at the residence. These were all relatives of the Whites. The tape was turned in of the interview with Burke and a transcript is available for review of the interview.

Det. Idler and I then transported Burke and the two Fernie children to ████ at the request of the Ramsey family. ████ is the address of the ████ residence. On arrival at the residence we were met by ████ who took custody of the children and escorted them inside the residence. Ofc. Morgan was also at the residence. We were told that Patsy and John Ramsey were inside the residence also.

INDEX

Note: Page numbers in *italics* refer to
photographs and documents.

A

ABC News, 34, 37, 42
Ainsworth, Steve, 84
Albuquerque Journal, 34
Arndt, Linda
  in charge of crime scene, 12–14
  police reports by, 182, *183–199*,
    200, *201–202*
  Ramsey interviews by, 113–114
  "Ramseys didn't act right" reported
    by, 71–73, *72*
  ransom note given to Ramseys by,
    48–49
Atler, Marilyn Van Derbur, 38–39
Aurora Police Department, 17, 56
autopsy
  cause of death established by, 66–67
  neck markings, 49–51, *50*
  no prior sexual abuse established by,
    39, 68–69
  people present at, 65
  stomach contents, 110–111, *111–*
    112
  stun gun use evidence, 67–68, *68*

B

Bardach, Ann Louise, 45–52
beauty pageants, 21–22, 37–38, 145,
  158–159
Beckner, Mark, 17–18
bedwetting motive, 16, 66–67, 118–119
Bode Labs, 92, 93, 129–130
books, about the case, 16, 118, 141–142
Boulder Daily Camera, 27, 38, 41, 113
Boulder Department of Social Services,
  109, 125

Boulder District Attorney's office
  autopsy attendance by, 66
  DNA evidence and, 19, 90, 92, *126–*
    127, 128–131
  exoneration of the Ramseys by, 19,
    93, *126–127*, 129–132, *173–177*
  Governor Romer and, 18, 47, 124
  grand jury and, 18, 47, 122–125
  Hunter as district attorney, 18. *See*
    also Hunter, Alex
  Hunter-Lacy comparison, 128–129
  incest theory pursued by, 39, *40*, 69
  influence on media, 35, 39, *40*, 46–
    47, 136–137
  Lacy as district attorney, 19, 93, 119,
    126–127, 128–132
  Lacy's successors, 132
  Ramsey (John Bennett) on the han-
    dling of case by, 2
  on Ramsey interviews, 117
  on ransom note, 46–47
  Smit and, 14–15, *31*, 93–94, 122–
    124, *123*
  on Thomas's book, 16
Boulder Police Department
  autopsy attendance by, 65
  criticism by federal judge, 119
  decision of guilt by, 55–56
  district attorney's removal of case
    from, 128
  district attorney's return of case to,
    132
  DNA evidence and, 22–24, *23*, 88–
    95, *91*
  false information leaked by, 22–26,
    23, 33–34, 35, 39–44, *43*, 55–56,
    93, 113, 135–136
  on footprint evidence, 11, 42–44,
    43, 75–76, *75*

help offered by other police departments, 17, 56, 133–134
incest theory pursued by, 39, *40*, 69
inexperience with homicides, ix, 11,
12, 14, 15, 16, 17, 18, 56, 90
initial investigation failures, 10–17,
55, 65, 71–73, 77–78
on JonBenét's stomach contents,
110–111, *111–112*
missed Ramsey interview opportunities, 114–116
police chief's failures, 17, 35, 52
police report documents, 178, *179–
181*, 182, *183–199, 201–202, 204*
police report summaries, *72*, 97, *98–
108*, 110–111, *111–112*
Ramsey (John Andrew) on mishan-
dling of case by, 147–148
Ramsey (John Bennett) on mishan-
dling of case by, 2–4, 5, 35–36
Ramsey interviews by, 97, 113–117
on ransom note, 51–52, 69, 82,
85
Smit and, 14–15, 93–94
on stun gun use, 67
Vanity Fair errors and, 45–46, 48–
49, 51–52
Brennan, Charlie, 134–136
Burke, Patrick, 48, 54

C
Campos, Paul, 131–132
Carnes, Julie E., 118–119
The Case of JonBenét (documentary), 35
CBI (Colorado Bureau of Investigation),
67, 90–92, *91*, 130
CBS News, 26, 33, 34, 37, 38–39, 52,
117–118
CellMark Labs, 92
Charlevoix (Michigan), 97, *155, 160*
Cherry Hills Village murder case, 87–88
circumstantial evidence, 69, 77–78
CNN, 27, 33, 34, 37
CODIS data bank, 92, 93
Colorado Bureau of Investigation (CBI),
67, 90–92, *91*, 130

Colorado Springs Gazette, 41
crime scene
"first witness as first suspect,"
61
house layout and size, *57–60*, 62,
63–64, 65
location of JonBenét body, 62
mistakes made at, 10–17, 55, 65,
77–78
police report documents, 22, *23*,
178, *179–181*, 182, *183–199*, 200,
201–202, 203, *204*

D
The Daily News (New York), 25, 26, 34
DeAngelo, Joseph, 88
The Death of Innocence (Ramsey & Ramsey), 118
Denver Police Department, 17, 56,
133–134
Denver Post, 35, 38, 131, 136–137
Dirty Harry (film), 84
Discovery+, 142
district attorney's office. *See* Boulder
District Attorney's office
DNA evidence, 86–95
as answer to murderer's identity, 7,
86
Boulder District Attorney's office
and, 19, 90, 92, *126–127*, 128–
131
Boulder Police Department and, 86,
88–95, *91*
collection from Ramsey family, 22–
24, *23*
exoneration of the Ramseys by, 19,
90, 92, 93, 126–132
genetic DNA comparison possibility,
86–88
other possibilities for, 95
Smit DNA team analysis, 93–94
test results, 89–93, *89, 91*, 129–130
"touch DNA" testing, 92–93, 129–
130
Dobersen, Michael, 67–68
documentaries, 35, 141, 142

doors
  open, 28–29
  pry marks on, 27–28
Dougherty, Michael, 132
Durgin, Leslie, 27, 33–35

E
Eller, John, 15–16, 116
evidence of intruder. *See also* DNA
  evidence
  circumstantial, 77–78
  force entry signs, 27–30, *30–32*, 33,
    48, *48*, 54, 69–70
  no prior sexual abuse evidence, 39,
    68–69
  pubic hair, 76
  ransom note wording, 83–85
  shoe imprints, 75–76, *75*
evidence possibly implicating the Ramseys, 57–78. *See also* ransom note
  about: overview, 61
  attorneys hired for Ramsey as, 74
  blanket around body, 70
  circumstantial evidence, 69, 77–78
  "first witness as first suspect," 61
  house layout and size, *57–60*, 62,
    63–64, 65, 73–74
  lack of similar crimes, 71
  neighbor report of child's cream, 73–
    74
  911 call audio speculations, 74
  paintbrush as garrote, 74
  Patsy's outfit at the crime scene, 70
  "Ramseys didn't act right" theory,
    71–73, *72*
  ransom note, 41–42, 46–47, 51, 69.
    See also ransom note

F
Facebook, 139–140
federal judge ruling, 117–119
footprints, 11, 42–44, *43*, 75–76, *75*
forced entry
  evidence of intruder, 27–30, *30–32*,
    33, 69–70
  misinformation, 42–44, *43*
forums (online), 139–142

French, Rick, 10–11, 46, 113–114, 178,
  179–181
fruit cocktail, 111, *111–112*
Furman, Patrick, 48, 54

G
Garnett, Stan, 132
Golden State Killer, 88
Gosage, Ron, *23*, 88–90
grand jury hearing, 18, 47, 120–125,
  123
Greenwood, Ian, 140, 141

H
Haddon, Hal, 49, 130–131
Harsanyi, David, 131
HiTec footprint, 75–76, *75*
house layout and size, *57–60*, 62, *63–
  64*, 65
Hunter, Alex
  criticism of, 16, 17–18
  grand jury hearing and, 18, 47, 122–
    125, *123*
  plea bargains and, 128
  on possible arrest of John, 136–137
  on Ramsey interviews, 117
  on ransom note author, *46*–47
  on Thomas's book, 16
  update on, 125

I
incest theory, 38–40, *40*, 69
insider insights, 133–138
Instagram, 141
intruder. *See* evidence of intruder

J
JonBenét Ramsey: The List (documentary), 142
JonBenét Ramsey: What Really Happened
  (documentary), 142

K
Ketchum, Sue, 67
Koby, Tom, 17, 33, 52, 133–134

L
Lacy, Mary Keenan, 19, 92–93, 119,
   126–127, 128–132, *173–177*
Lindbergh, Charles, 71
Lindbergh kidnapping, 71

M
Marra, Cindy, 94
Mason, Larry, 114, 200
metal grate evidence, 29–30, 48, 54,
   69–70
Meyer, John, 66, 67, 68
Michaud, Dave, 133–134
Morgan, Bryan, 130–131

N
NBC News, 27, 34, 37, 69
neighbors' observations, 28, 29, 73–74
Newsweek Magazine, 37
Nick of Time (film), 84–85
911 call, 9, 74

O
ongoing publicity. *See* publicity
   (ongoing)
online coverage, 139

P
pageants, 21–22, 37–38, 145, *158–159*
paintbrush, as evidence, 74, 118
Patterson, Fred, 13, 14, 113–114, 203,
   204
physical evidence. *See* autopsy; DNA
   evidence; evidence of intruder;
   evidence possibly implicating the Ramseys
pineapple, 110–111, *110–112*
police reports. *See* Boulder Police
   Department
pry marks, 27–28
pubic hair, 76
publicity (first week), 20–36
   about: overview, x
   false information, 22–26, *23*, 27,
      33–35, 135, 136
   headlines, x, 22, 25–26, 135

   homicide detective's perspective on,
      24–25, 26
   on JonBenét's pageants, 21–22
   Ramsey (John Andrew) on, 35–36
   against the Ramseys, 21–22, 24–26,
      33
publicity (ongoing), 37–56, 139–142
   books about the case, x, 16, 118,
      141–142
   decision of guilt influencing, 54–56
   documentaries about the case, 35,
      141, 142
   false information, 39–44, *43*, 55–56,
      93, 113, 135–136
   headlines, 52–54, 75, 135
   on JonBenét's pageants, 37–38
   social media coverage, 139–141
   Vanity Fair errors, 45–52, *48*, 54

Q
Quayle, Sylvia, 87–88

R
Ramsey, Beth, 4, 7, 147
Ramsey, Burke
   accusations against, 125
   bedroom location, 65
   exoneration of, 90, 92, 130
   lawsuits by, 117–118
   long-term effect of case on, 6–7
   moves following death of JonBenét, 5
   911 call audio and, 74
   photographs, *96*, *149*, *157*
   police interviews, 114
   Social Services evaluation of, 109
Ramsey, Jan, *1*, 2, 6, 7, 8, 146–147
Ramsey, John Andrew
   arrival at crime scene, 51
   on the Boulder brand, 137–138
   Brennan's apology to, 134–136
   on case's effect on his father, 7–8, 146
   on current status of case, 147–148
   on false accusations against his
      family, 35–36
   on JonBenét, 144–145
   long-term effect of case on, 3, 6, 147

personal qualities, 135–136

Ramsey, John Bennett. *See also* evidence possibly implicating the Ramseys
  accused of flying a plane before funeral, 47
  accused of money complaints, 48
  attorneys hired for, 48
  background and history of, 97, *98–108*
  on Burke, 6–7
  The Death of Innocence, 118
  DNA collection from, 22, *23*
  exoneration of, 19, 90, 92, 93, *126–127*, 129–132, *173–177*
  on faith and spirituality, 4
  on the "good officers," 4
  grand jury and, 121, 125
  on JonBenét's pageants, 145
  lawsuits, 117–118
  long-term effect of case on, 2–3, 6, 7–8, 146–147, 148
  marriage to Jan, 2–3, 6
  moves following death of JonBenét, 5, 6–7
  on murderer's identity, 7
  on Patsy, 6
  on peace, 4–5
  photographs, *1, 20, 96, 153*
  police file demands by, 48–49
  police interviews, 113–117
  politics and, 5
  publicity during first week against, 25–26
  quest for justice, 3–4
  ransom note suspicions, 41, 46–47, 69
  suspicious behavior reported by district attorney, 47

Ramsey, JonBenét
  bedroom location, 62, *64*, 65
  cause of death, 66–67
  details of death, 21, 47, 49–51, *50*
  evidence in bedroom, 76
  evidence on body of, 75–77
  location of body, 29, 55, 62, 70

  pageants and, 21–22, 37–38, 145, *158–159*
  personal items of, *143, 161–163*
  personal qualities, 144–148
  photographs, *96*, 143, *149–160*
  staging of death accusations, 49–51, *50*

Ramsey, Melinda Bennett, 22, *23*, 51

Ramsey, Patricia "Patsy." *See also* evidence possibly implicating the Ramseys
  accused of spending too much money, 48
  attorneys hired for, 48
  background and history of, 97, *98–108*
  bedwetting motive attributed to, 16, 66–67, 118–119
  body and DNA collection from, 22–24, *23*
  death of, 2, 7, 134
  The Death of Innocence, 118
  exoneration of, 19, 90, 92, 93, *126–127*, 129–132, *173–177*
  faith of, 134
  grand jury and, 121, 125
  on JonBenét's pageants, 145
  lawsuits, 117–118
  moves following death of JonBenét, 5, 6–7
  911 call, 9, 74
  ovarian cancer diagnosis, 24, 145
  personal qualities of, 6
  photographs, *20, 96, 154, 156*
  police file demands by, 48–49
  police interviews, 113–117
  publicity during first week on, 21, 22, 24–26
  ransom note and, 41–42, 51
  suspicious behavior reported by police, 46

Ramsey Murder Book Summary Index, 97, *98–108*, *111–112*

Ransom (film), 84, 85

ransom note
  Boulder District Attorney's office on, 46–47